Providing Hyper-Localized Early Childhood Programming

This important and engaging resource offers a step-by-step framework for developing early childhood community programming that centers the learning needs of children, supersedes socioeconomic barriers, and activates the power of community.

The book centers on an in-depth exploration of the Early Learning Neighborhood Collaborative (ELNC), a place-based, early learning collaborative that provides funding, innovative shared support services, and advocacy to partner organizations rooted in vulnerable communities, with the primary goal of readying children for the first day of kindergarten. The author details the concept and practice of a place-based intentional preschool system, including the lessons that were learned through the creation of ELNC and how it successfully prepares children of color for success in school and beyond. The program uses a two-generation approach in which families are coached to address barriers that keep them from being their child's first teachers and are supported in navigating community resources.

Through the insightful model this book provides, education leaders and early childhood teachers can learn more about emerging best practices in community programming, identify ways to adapt the ELNC model and test it in their current programming, and use the ELNC process to change their own neighborhoods for the better.

Dr. Nkechy Ekere Ezeh is a tenured professor of education at Aquinas College and the founder and pedagogical leader of the landmark Early Learning Neighborhood Collaborative (ELNC)—an umbrella organization for six grass-roots intuitions of trust vested in ensuring that vulnerable children and families have access to place-based, culturally competent, quality early learning opportunities. In 2012, Dr. Ezeh developed Empowering Parents Impacting Children (EPIC)® as the main component of its two-generational approach. This EPIC model is one that empowers parents to take back their role as a leader and their child's first teacher. Dr. Ezeh also founded Urban Core Collective (formerly Anchor Organization Network) that has an "indigenous leadership path" as one of their scopes of work.

Providing Hyper-Localized Early Childhood Programming

A Framework from the Early Learning Neighborhood Collaborative (ELNC)

Nkechy Ekere Ezeh

Designed cover image: Onyinye Ezeh Kelly

First published 2024
by Routledge
605 Third Avenue, New York, NY 10158

and by Routledge
4 Park Square, Milton Park, Abingdon, Oxon, OX14 4RN

Routledge is an imprint of the Taylor & Francis Group, an informa business

© 2024 Nkechy Ekere Ezeh

The right of Nkechy Ekere Ezeh to be identified as author of this work has been asserted in accordance with sections 77 and 78 of the Copyright, Designs and Patents Act 1988.

All rights reserved. No part of this book may be reprinted or reproduced or utilised in any form or by any electronic, mechanical, or other means, now known or hereafter invented, including photocopying and recording, or in any information storage or retrieval system, without permission in writing from the publishers.

Trademark notice: Product or corporate names may be trademarks or registered trademarks, and are used only for identification and explanation without intent to infringe.

Library of Congress Cataloging-in-Publication Data
Names: Ezeh, Nkechy (Nkechy Ekere), author.
Title: Localized early childhood programming: framework from the early learning neighborhood collaborative (ELNC)/Nkechy Ekere Ezeh.
Description: New York, NY: Routledge, 2023. |
Includes bibliographical references and index. |
Identifiers: LCCN 2022052703 (print) | LCCN 2022052704 (ebook) |
ISBN 9781032386409 (hardback) | ISBN 9781032377780 (paperback) |
ISBN 9781003346012 (ebook)
Subjects: LCSH: Early Learning Neighborhood Collaborative. | Early childhood education—Michigan—Grand Rapids. | Community education—Michigan—Grand Rapids. | Educational equalization—Michigan—Grand Rapids.
Classification: LCC LB1139.27.M47 E94 2023 (print) |
LCC LB1139.27.M47 (ebook) | DDC 372.2109774—dc23/eng/20230118
LC record available at https://lccn.loc.gov/2022052703
LC ebook record available at https://lccn.loc.gov/2022052704

ISBN: 9781032386409 (hbk)
ISBN: 9781032377780 (pbk)
ISBN: 9781003346012 (ebk)

DOI: 10.4324/9781003346012

Typeset in Palatino
by codeMantra

This book is dedicated to Black and Brown children of ELNC and their families who are often left out of the educational system and to my very own children Onyinye Mk., Obinna, Akuezumkpa, Nnenna, and Nkechy-Nicole who unknowingly became my child development laboratory subjects that inspired my academic and professional work.

Edited by Dr. Nalova Westbrook

Contents

Foreword viii
Preface xi

Introduction 1

1 The ELNC model 9

2 Leadership 49

3 Collaboration: partnering with parents, partnering with place-based organizations 66

4 Values 83

5 What is child development? 106

6 Guiding principles: what ELNC believes about children 119

7 Looking forward 139

   Appendix A:
   About our founding collaborative partner organizations 149
   About the community experts quoted in this book 152

   Appendix B: ELNC report card 2010–2015 160

   Index 179

Foreword

The early years are a sensitive period of children's development. These years are even more critical for Black and Latinx children, multilingual and multidialectal children, children with various cognitive and physical needs, and children growing up in poverty. Unfortunately, data continues to show the unevenness in children's access and experiences in early childhood based on their social or economic status (i.e., race, place, ethnicity, gender, household income, disability) or both. Nationhood cannot be built on neglect. Longitudinal research reveals over and over the emotional, academic, and employment success of adults based on in part quality early childhood education (ECE). Accordingly, social and economic inequities can't continue if we mean to maximize the potential of our society, which requires that all children are *protected* from harm, trauma, and material hardship; societal well-being also requires that the health, wealth, and educational excellence of all children is *promoted* and that children's cultural identity and language are preserved as part of school readiness programs. This book, ***Providing Hyper-Localized Early Childhood Programming: A Framework from the Early Learning Neighborhood Collaborative (ELNC)*** by Dr. Nkechy Ekere Ezeh, conveys the possibility of re-visioning what early education can be in the United States and around the globe when we center the rights of children, underscore families as the first teacher in partnership with ECE stakeholders, value educators and staff, and involve the community such as churches and ethnic centers.

The story of the Early Learning Neighborhood Collaborative is the story of Dr. Ezeh—a Black woman, a mother, an African immigrant, and her experience in a world dominated by white people, especially white women, and how her presence was not well received by those in power. Dr. Ezeh uncovers the often under- or unacknowledged barriers in the United States to access to early childhood education—racism and class. More importantly, she shows us the importance of dreaming and activating the power of community by changing the faces and voices of those who are identified to be ECE leaders. Dr. Ezeh shows us a glimmer of what North America's equitable early learning can be when fully activated and supported.

Iheoma U. Iruka, Ph.D.
Research Professor, Department of Public Policy
Fellow, Frank Porter Graham Child Development Institute
Founding Director, Equity Research Action Coalition

The City of Grand Rapids is one of the hidden jewels in the United States. Culture, history, and innovation abound. Grand Rapids constantly evolves and adapts to the challenges of an urban center. Notwithstanding such qualities, there are harsh realities of historically-rooted social and economic inequities that create hardships for the city's most vulnerable citizens who are overwhelmingly Black and Brown. Race and poverty are the culprits. Race and poverty in Grand Rapids are very real determinants of basic quality of life. The Early Learning Neighborhood Collaborative (ELNC) is a true grassroots organization that arose to meet a need verified by real data collected over a sustained period of time. ELNC serves as an example of what happens when courage, collaborative thinking, vision, and financial resources are collectively employed to undermine racial strife. The city's narrative of children living in the urban core who were not ready for day one of kindergarten became the catalyst for institution-building. If there were no ELNC, this negative school readiness narrative would remain an adverse impact on the city's progeny and quality of Grand Rapids' labor force. As a proud partner whose been here from the beginning of the organization's development, I believe the ELNC and Grand Rapids story has yet to be told enough, thoroughly. The narrative in *Providing Hyper-Localized Early Childhood Programming: A Framework from the Early Learning Neighborhood Collaborative (ELNC)* weakens the zip code and household income relationship: where a child lives does not have to be a barrier to a foundation for lifelong learning and economic vitality. Every ELNC preschool graduation, some of which are the first of any kind in a household, convey the message that investment in children and families are critical to the success of Grand Rapids and any other city.

Rev. Howard C. Earle, Jr., D.Min.

Preface

Friends and family have told me for a long time now that I should publish a book on, and tell the story of, the Early Learning Neighborhood Collaborative (ELNC). After hearing the stories about ELNC, family and friends always wanted to know more. So, without further ado, I took your advice and the story of ELNC is in print! *Providing Hyper-Localized Early Childhood Programming: A Framework from the Early Learning Neighborhood Collaborative (ELNC).* This is our story. It is not perfect, but it gives you great insight into what it took for us get this landmark early childhood education work started. Early Learning Neighborhood Collaborative (ELNC) is a trusted, place-based, early learning collaborative with projects in three Michigan cities—Grand Rapids, Battle Creek, and Kalamazoo. ELNC provides funding, innovative shared support services, and advocacy to partner organizations rooted in vulnerable communities with the primary goal of getting children ready for kindergarten day one!

ELNC work is NOT easy by any means, but it is gratifying to see the children every May or June in their graduation gowns and hoods receiving their "diplomas" with their entire family members beaming with pride because they did it! These brilliant learners completed rigorous, research-based preschool. They dispelled any negative myths about the academic achievement of Black and Brown, low-income children. The single event of preschool graduation each year brings on hope for more graduations to come and the confirmation for our families who were once ruled out as "bad" parents that they are not bad after all. The only bad thing is societal perceptions of such loving, dedicated parents.

Despite much progress, figuring out a system that prioritizes the learning needs of our vulnerable children and their loving, dedicated parents, forging strong partnerships our foundation suddenly shifted as a global pandemic caused the world to be put on pause. ELNC marshalled its efforts to address the impact this would have on pre-primary school education of Black and Brown families in the Covid era. COVID-19's impact on ELNC includes but is not limited to:

Our children: As I write this preface 17 October 2022, we at ELNC are now seeing the impact of the pandemic on infants and toddlers—children who were either born during the pandemic or were infants when it began. Many have been confined to their home environment with little or no contact with anyone other than their immediate family members. Subsequent access to the broader outside world meant interactions with face masks as opposed to faces. Social distancing replaced handshakes, hugs, and other human touch. The originally home-bound infants and toddlers could not see facial expressions or observe other body language from human interactions when riding in a stroller with their parents through Grand Rapids, Battle Creek, or Kalamazoo neighborhoods. With a few exceptions, all of our classrooms have two or more children who are exhibiting social behaviors that require individualized attention. Such a trend is unprecedented.

Our Staff: A significant teacher shortage exists locally and nationally, exacerbated by COVID-19 restrictions. Pre-COVID teachers stayed home during the pandemic to take care of their own children whose schools were closed. Now they are reluctant to return to the classroom as there are other available jobs with higher wages and benefits or they have just decided to stay home. This fact coupled with the need for an additional teacher in the classroom to support the increase in the number of children with special needs, makes the teacher shortage a critical threat to ensuring that our Black and Brown children have access to quality early childhood education programs. Currently, most ELNC site directors are also in the classroom due to lack of staffing which also has a negative effect on their ability to ensure that quality and licensing standards are met.

Our Pay: ELNC is firmly committed to ensuring that early childhood education teacher's remuneration structure is competitive—whether employees or employers are driving the market. This is made more difficult when funding has not been increased at the same rate as wages have increased.

ELNC has several vacant positions to which few or no jobseekers have applied. With the current job market, the organization is paying competitive wages and increasing benefits. ELNC has also adopted the following solutions to adverse Covid-related impact on pay: (1) providing capacity-building funds to partners for recruitment and training of additional administrative staff; (2) updating infrastructure that includes improvements in technology; (3) adding more family coaches to support sites serving an increased number of high needs families who are dealing with pandemic challenges.

Nonetheless, our partners are drowning. They do not have the internal capacity to address the increasing demands on administrative staff. Staff are sometimes assuming two or three staff positions.

The importance of strong technology infrastructure has never been more necessary. ZOOM meetings, virtual classrooms, data collection and more are pushing technology limits.

Families are struggling—family coaches are more involved in supporting health needs, attendance, and referrals than before.

Despite these and other Covid-related challenges impacting our children, our staff, and our pay, ELNC has overwhelming support from various community stakeholders who value primary school readiness success. Evidence you will read about in this book reveals the overwhelming positive impact of ELNC on children and society. The numbers do not lie, so philanthropic funding for ELNC continues to mount. As you will read in subsequent chapters, the data shows how essential the Early Learning Neighborhood Collaborative is to families in West Michigan. Our children meet or exceed local district, state, national, and even international learning benchmarks. So we anticipate ELNC's growth and development far beyond the neighborhoods we serve.

Even as hard as it is to navigate the impact of a global pandemic, it is my hope that this book calls you to challenge social and economic hierarchies across communities. Our calling in this world is historical and sociological. We aim to attack racism and poverty for betterment of our vulnerable children—especially our Black and Brown Children for many generations to come!

Introduction

The year 2009 is a critical year for providing hyper-localized early childhood education (ECE) programming. The City of Grand Rapids, in the Midwestern region of the United States, discovered that 83% of children slated to enter public city schools were not ready for kindergarten learning (Russell, 2009). These kids are what the field of education might call "struggling learners" (Anderson, 1981; Benner, 2009, 2010; Burns et al., 1998; Fountas & Pinnell, 2009; Gaskins, 2005; Henriques, 2021; Lienemann et al., 2013; Martin, 2008; Martin & Daniels, 2018; Minskoff, 2005; Porton, 2012; Radencich & McKay, 1995; Smith & MacLeod-Vidal, 2022; Taylor, 2004; Tovani, 2004; Wright, 2014). In other words, these very young learners were reading below one or more grade levels. Granted, in early childhood, all learners are initially in the visual world (Bronson, 1974; Piaget & Cook, 1957). Children at this stage of development do not often recognize alpha-numeric code in part because sensorimotor and preoperational reasoning, which are composed of manipulating objects and thinking by perception, dominate. But research (Byrne & Fielding-Barnsley, 1989; Crain-Thoreson & Dale, 1992; Kaderavek & Justice, 2005) is clear that kids should enter kindergarten at least with a certain level of language and neuro power to learn the ABCs as well as to learn number identification.

The unfortunate reality of the 83% statistic is that the Grand Rapids early learning ecosystem reflects a larger phenomenon in many cities throughout the country. Racism, segregation, and poverty found across the United States, as Kozol (2006) observes, and even internationally are rampant in the Midwestern city. These are structural conditions that have a direct effect on the ability

DOI: 10.4324/9781003346012-1

of some children to school. "This is a national crisis," says Dana Boals, founding board chair of the Early Learning Neighborhood Collaborative (ELNC). Boals understands the importance of ECE as a requisite condition for success later in life. "There's a sense of urgency. You've only got two years to prepare children to be successful in kindergarten day one—you've got to do it right." Due to limited funding, by the time children came to ELNC at age 3, there was approximately two years to prepare them for primary school. Doing "it right" means providing early learners with nurturing home and preschool environments that allow for brain, language, and physical development (Lim et al., 2022).

Independent consultant Sharon Killebrew agrees that racism, segregation, and poverty undermine child development. "If they're not ready to start learning when they enter kindergarten, there's no magical switch that happens," she observes. "They're always behind." Killebrew's sentiments reflect a basic maxim across the ECE scholar landscape. The achievement gap (Ansell, 2011; Burchinal et al., 2011; Friedman-Krauss et al., 2016) starts before kindergarten as a result of structural barriers that the Grand Rapids community has been facing since at least, according to Randal Jelks (2006), the 1900 northern migration of Black people out of the southern part of the country. The 83% figure of learners in the city under or unprepared for kindergarten is ostensibly a historical inequity.

Notwithstanding, Grand Rapids has not been alone in trying to solve the achievement and preparation gap problem. Leaders beyond city walls had for years used philanthropic work to bolster ECE. Money from various public and private stakeholders such as Kent County and Dollar General Literacy Foundation (Kramer & Windram, 2018; Moody, 2018) have poured in, experts convened meetings, but the city's children were not adequately being served. A positive change in achievement had yet to be realized. The numbers do not lie. Strategic city and other stakeholder leadership efforts did not yield results in school success for vulnerable children. The historical constraints of racism and poverty appeared too strong, even insurmountable.

The reality of segregation is real—In fact, segregation is the culprit. Segregation in Grand Rapids, as elsewhere, aimed to hide the truth of the deep structural problems in schools. "Segregation makes it easier for white people to not even be aware of their neighbor's needs," notes Pastor Howard Earle Jr., a local Pastor and a collaborative partner with ELNC.

> If you ask a middle class family with employment and earning potential, they may say Grand Rapids is a great place for a family. But if you ask the economically challenged families, especially the non-white families, there would be a completely different sentiment. And there's all kind of data that supports that claim.

Robin DiAngelo (2018) and Ijeoma Oluo's (2019) research supports Pastor Earle's observations. These two scholars explain that racism sets up even seemingly progressive whites to overlook, ignore, deny, and defend racial inequities. The "fragility of whiteness," particularly in the United States, centers on rejecting the fact that racism exists or if it does that individual whites are not responsible. Pastor Earle's observation about lack of awareness among whites in Grand Rapids about racial segregation is what DiAngelo and Oluo would say whites in Grand Rapids view as a legal and institutional problem and not as a personal one. Such a view allows middle class and affluent whites in the city to go about their daily lives without any empathetic action to undo the economic and educational depression of Black and Brown neighbors living in poverty. On the other hand, Pastor Earle, a Black male engineer by trade who answered a call to serve as an ecclesiastical leader, has a keen understanding of the effects of segregation on the quality of life for Black people and other folk of color in Grand Rapids. Clearly, Pastor Earle is aware that segregation allows the city community to downplay the 83% statistic of underprepared learners for kindergarten because the 83% of underprepared learners are just not part of the middle class and affluent white experience in Grand Rapids. Segregation, exacerbated by white fragility, allows certain segments of the city area population to be unaware of, ignore, and overlook race in schools and other institutions.

At some point, though, ignoring such staggering statistics revealing the toll of race on early learning could not continue. Brave funders and leaders began to pay attention to the learning disparity data. The gravity of the problem – that less than one in four children were ready for kindergarten – was finally blatant enough racial segregation for some whites in power and their allies to face the root causes and approach problem-solving differently. Undoubtedly, there was an urgent need for new solutions.

New problem-solving approaches to old problems required bringing in new people. The obvious choice was someone with an early childhood education (ECE) background as well as with robust academic knowledge of structural inequalities. Nkechy Ekere Ezeh, Ed. D. became the figurehead because of her track record of addressing ECE questions through the lens of racism and segregation. In addition, Ezeh offered unique personal experience as someone originally from Nigeria who has lived in Grand Rapids with her family the majority of her adult life. As a Black immigrant with deep ties to the city, Ezeh has brought an indigenous leader (Ezeh, 2022) and international perspective to hyper-localized early childhood programming. But more than impressive credentials and lived experience, Ezeh has proven herself to be a champion for poor Black and Brown kids by challenging the status quo. Ezeh has been willing to push back to those in positions of power to help her Grand Rapids community have those uncomfortable conversations about the role of race in early learning (Blackson et al., 2022). For Ezeh, Black and Brown children deserve intellectual and policy approaches that would not ignore their lived material realities.

Cash-strapped Black and Brown children also deserve leaders who believe in the capacity for success of all children. Educationists are fond of saying "all children can learn" (Leverett, 2006). But then educators often do not create the conditions for everyone to actually learn (Thomas & Bainbridge, 2019). And those without an educationist background can be most ignorant to the learning needs of children (Noguera, 2012). Grand Rapids, like many cities in the United States, was in need of leaders who believed all children – regardless of neighborhood, family history, or financial status – were born ready to learn.

Accordingly, solving early learning problems in Grand Rapids was, first and foremost, a matter of a shift in paradigms. Leaders needed to move from ability to access mindsets. Ezeh began the work by gathering others around her who also knew that the truth was access and not ability. The founding board chair of ELNC was one of those with an empowering outlook. "We have everything we need here, right here in our neighborhoods of color, for success for our children," opines Boals. Boals's words reveal that, contrary to popular belief, achievement gaps in early learning and in the later years are not necessarily an issue of lack of resources. For Boals, everything has been available – from people to money to furniture to kids' building blocks. Boals's words also divulge the city community perhaps did not believe they had everything they needed to provide quality, equitable learning to all children. It took an immigrant perspective to tap into existing local resources to provide equitable early learning for the neighborhood.

Pastor Earle echoes the belief of Dana Boals. He has seen the incredible success that ELNC's strategy and values bring to the children in his community because Pastor Earle believes in the power of collective effort. He knows that the statistics that motivated the W. K. Kellogg Foundation, Ezeh, and the collaborative she gathered will merely open more doors for community development, including successful early learning for poor Black and Brown children. According to Pastor Earle, the city does not need to move children from one part of town to another. "Zip code," he maintains, "does not have to define a child's future." Busing kids from one neighborhood to another was a strategy of the 1960s, 1970s, and 1980s that even continues today based on the theory that Black kids need to go to schools with white kids on the other side of town to get a quality education. These integrationist efforts in schools have had mixed results at best (Anderson, 1994). ELNC is anchored in the belief that Black and Brown communities provide all the ingredients to dismantle outdated, zip code-driven quality ECE. ELNC was founded on the premise that, although zip codes correlate with achievement scores, graduation rates, and other markers of successful schooling (Noguera, 2003), they don't have to.

References

Anderson, C. (1994). *Black labor, White wealth: The search for power and economic justice*. PowerNomics Corporation of America. Bethesda: Powernomics corporation of America.

Anderson, J. R. (1981). *Cognitive skills and their acquisition* (Carnegie Mellon Symposia on Cognition Series, 1st ed.). Symposium on Cognition, Collection of papers presented at the Sixteenth Annual Carnegie Symposium on Cognition. Pittsburgh, PA: Lawrence Erlbaum Associates.

Ansell, S. (2011, July 7). Achievement gap. *Education Week*. Retrieved August 23, 2022 from https://www.edweek.org/leadership/achievement-gap/2004/09

Benner, S. (2009). *Promising practices for elementary teachers: Make no excuses!* Corwin Press California, USA.

Benner, S. (2010). *Promising practices for elementary teachers: Make no excuses!* SAGE Publications.

Blackson, E. A., Gerdes, M., Segan, E., Anokam, C., & Johnson, T. J. (2022). Racial bias toward children in the early childhood education setting. *Journal of Early Childhood Research, 20*(3), 277–292.

Bronson, G. (1974). The postnatal growth of visual capacity. *Child Development, 45*(4), 873.

Burchinal, M., McCartney, K., Steinberg, L., Crosnoe, R., Friedman, S. L., McLoyd, V., & Pianta, R. (2011, July 25). Examining the Black-White achievement gap among low-income children using the NICHD study of early child care and youth development. *Child Development, 82*(5), 1404–1420.

Burns, M. S., Snow, C. E., Jenkins, P. D., & Griffin, P. (1998). *Preventing reading difficulties in young children*. Washington, DC: National Academies Press.

Byrne, B., & Fielding-Barnsley, R. (1989). Phonemic awareness and letter knowledge in the child's acquisition of the alphabetic principle. *Journal of Educational Psychology, 81*(3), 313.

Crain-Thoreson, C., & Dale, P. S. (1992). Do early talkers become early readers? Linguistic precocity, preschool language, and emergent literacy. *Developmental Psychology, 28*(3), 421.

DiAngelo, R. (2018). *White fragility: Why it's so hard for white people to talk about racism* (Reprint ed.). Boston, MA: Beacon Press.

Ezeh, N. (2022). *Leading while learning* [Unpublished manuscript].

Fountas, I. C., & Pinnell, G. S. (2009). *Fountas and Pinnell Leveled Literacy Intervention (LLI) Orange (Grade K) program guide*. Portsmouth, NH: Heinemann.

Friedman-Krauss A., Barnett W. S., & Nores M. (2016). *How much can high-quality universal pre-K reduce achievement gaps?* Washington, DC: Center for American Progress/New Brunswick, NJ: National Institute on Early Education Research. Retrieved from https://nieer.org/wp-content/uploads/2017/01/NIEER-AchievementGaps-report.pdf

Gaskins, I. W. (2005). *Success with struggling readers: The Benchmark School approach*. New York, NY: Guilford Publications.

Henriques, D. (2021). *Bridging the gap—parents guide for struggling learners in elementary school*. Independently Published.

Jelks, R. M. (2006). *African Americans in the furniture city: The struggle for civil rights in grand rapids* (Illustrated ed.). Champaign, IL: University of Illinois Press.

Kaderavek, J. N., & Justice, L. M. (2005). The effect of book genre in the repeated readings of mothers and their children with language impairment: A pilot investigation. *Child Language Teaching and Therapy*, *21*(1), 75–92.

Kozol, J. (2006). *The shame of the nation: The restoration of apartheid schooling in America* (Reprint ed.). New York, NY: Crown.

Kramer, A., & Windram, H. (2018, October 25). The ready by five early childhood millage for Kent county. *Chamber Blog*. Retrieved August 24, 2022 from https://www.grandrapids.org/blog/advocacy-government-affairs/ready-five-early-childhood-millage-kent-county/

Leverett, L. (2006, September 5). Closing the achievement gap: "All children can learn". *Edutopia*. Retrieved September 5, 2006 from https://www.edutopia.org/closing-achievement-gap

Lienemann, T. O., Hagaman, J. L., & Reid, R. (2013). *Strategy instruction for students with learning disabilities* (2nd ed.). New York, NY: Guilford Publications.

Lim, S., Levickis, P., & Eadie, P. (2022). Associations between Early Childhood Education and Care (ECEC) attendance, adversity and language outcomes of 2-year-olds. *Journal of Early Childhood Research*. https://journals.sagepub.com/doi/abs/10.1177/1476718X221087078

Martin, K., & Daniels, C. (2018). *Navigating a teacher's first year*. Peoria, AZ: Perfect Bound Marketing.

Martin, L. C. (2008). *Strategies for teaching students with learning disabilities*. Thousand Oaks, CA: SAGE Publications.

Minskoff, E. H. (2005). *Teaching reading to struggling learners*. Baltimore, MD: Brookes Publishing Co.

Moody, P. (2018, August 28). Dollar General Literacy Foundation awards $67K in Michigan for 2018. *Moodyonthemarket*. Retrieved August 23, 2022 from https://www.moodyonthemarket.com/dollar-general-literacy-foundation-awards-67k-in-michigan-for-2018/

Noguera, P. A. (2003). *City Schools and the American Dream: Reclaiming the promise of public education (Multicultural Education Series)* (Reprint ed.). New York, NY: Teachers College Press.

Noguera, P. (2012). The achievement gap and the schools we need: Creating the conditions where race and class no longer predict student achievement. Retrieved from https://www.shankerinstitute.org/sites/default/files/Noguera--The%20Achievement%20Gap%20and%20The%20Schools%20We%20Need.pdf

Oluo, I. (2019). *So you want to talk about race* (Reprint ed.). Cypress, CA: Seal Press.

Piaget, J., & Cook, M. (1957). *The construction of reality in the child*. New York, NY: Adfo Books.

Porton, H. D. (2012). *Helping struggling learners succeed in school*. Abingdon: Routledge.

Radencich, M. C., & McKay, L. J. (1995). *Flexible grouping for literacy in the elementary grades*. Des Moines, IA: Allyn and Bacon.

Russell, M. S. (2009). *GRPS school chief Bernard Taylor delivers 'State of Schools' address*. Retrieved from https://www.mlive.com/northeastadvance/2009/02/grps_school_chief_bernard_tayl.html

Smith, K., & MacLeod-Vidal, H. (2022). *Teach reading with Orton-Gillingham: Early reading skills: A companion guide with dictation activities, decodable passages, and other supplemental... struggling readers and students with Dyslexia*. Berkeley, CA: Ulysses Press.

Taylor, R. T. (2004). Using literacy leadership to improve the achievement of struggling students. *Middle School Journal*, *36*(1), 26–31.

Thomas, M. D., & Bainbridge, W. L. (2019, February 23). The truth about "All children can learn" (Opinion). *Education Week*. Retrieved from https://www.edweek.org/policy-politics/opinion-the-truth-about-all-children-can-learn/2000/12

Tovani, C. (2004). *Do I really have to teach reading? Content comprehension, grades 6–12* (1st ed.). Portsmouth, NH: Stenhouse Publishers.

Wright, J. (2014). *Strategies for struggling learners in the era of CCSS & RTI*. Lake Worth FL: National Professional Resources, Inc./Dude Publishing.

1

The ELNC model

By 2010, evidence was mounting that in Grand Rapids, Michigan, the current system of education was not working for certain segments of the population. Information had been circulating publicly for at least a year to the community, as mentioned in the introductory chapter, by then Grand Rapids Public Schools (GRPS) Superintendent Dr. Bernard Taylor, Jr. that 83% of entering kindergartners scored less than proficient in a composite of key literacy indicators. By proficient, the city means to say that approximately eight out of ten learners did not possess what some educationists might call standard level phonological, visual meaning, and other pre-alphabetic and letter recognition skills to begin primary school (Invernizzi et al., 2004; Leong & Haines, 1978).

In 2009, the four-year high-school graduation rates at the GRPS's district's alternative schools were telling: as low as 8% at Southeast Career Pathways. Graduation rates also wimped at the district's comprehensive high schools: 65% at Ottawa Hills, 71% at Central, 72% at Creston, and 74% at Union, respectively (Center for Educational Performance and Information, 2010). Research (Clerkin & Gilligan, 2018; Darney et al., 2013; Davoudzadeh et al., 2015; Duncan et al., 2007; Feinstein et al., 2007; Moore et al., 2014; Noguera, 2012; Smith & Glass, 2019; Watts et al., 2014) shows that many of these figures could be either predicted or strongly estimated based on learner readiness for primary school. There are longitudinal studies (Adams & Singh, 1998; Anthony & Ogg,

2019; Bar-Kochva & Nevo, 2019; Bembry et al., 1998; Bodovski & Youn, 2011; Munoz & Chang, 2007) that speak to this trend. And while there must be heavy investment in secondary and adult learning, it is widely accepted in education circles that learning success begins in the early years of school (Mariano et al., 2019). Ezeh took note of these abysmal graduation numbers but could only accept them as failure of society and not as failure of kids. Institutions fail students and not the other way around is common parlance among education academics and practitioners (Anderson, 1994; Freire & Macedo, 1987; Giroux, 2001; hooks, 1994; Kozol, 2006; McLaren, 2022; Noguera, 2003).

One solution to offset these weak graduate rates is to build and strengthen institutions, which is why ELNC is so critically important. The statistics identified above show education in Grand Rapids needs the help of ELNC. As a Professor of Early Childhood Education (ECE) at Aquinas College, Dr. Nkechy Ekere Ezeh keenly understood that kindergarten readiness was a first critical step in a child's pathway to be able to actualize their human potential and become a self-sufficient adult.

> The relationship between the skills with which children enter school and their later academic performance is strikingly similar. Research has shown that there is nearly a 90% probability that a child will remain a poor reader at the end of the fourth grade if the child is a poor reader at the end of the first grade. Knowledge of alphabet letters at entry into kindergarten is a strong predictor of reading ability in 10th grade.
>
> (Boyer, 1991)

Boyer's position underscores high-school teachers and administrators hope that preschool, kindergarten, and first-grade teachers and parents will do the necessary work so that secondary education does not center on remediation (Keesey et al., 2014). Focusing on early literacy and numeracy (Macmillan, 2009) in learner populations that have historically been failed by schools will result in performance on or above grade-level years later (Clerkin & Gilligan, 2018; Fuson et al., 2015; ten

Braak et al., 2022; Watts et al., 2014). Early literacy, particularly with the objective to undercut poverty, is a matter of social justice (Shannon, 2014). Grand Rapids had damning statistics showing the city community that too many children, because of race and poverty, were not prepared to succeed in school, and people were finally paying attention enough to be willing to make real structural changes (Melhuish & Gardiner, 2019; Melvin et al., 2022; Slot, 2018). The 83% statistic reverberated through conversations about how to achieve success for children not only in kindergarten but also, as Boyer highlights, in the 10th grade.

As a result, there was another statistic: in 2011, the year that the Early Learning Neighborhood Collaborative (ELNC) began, only two in ten children in Grand Rapids' most vulnerable neighborhoods had access to preschool. While this phenomenon may not have been unique to the city, such revelations were very disconcerting for stakeholders who care (Noddings, 2005; Swick et al., 2001). Based on the research of Ezeh and other ECE scholars, restoring access to preschool is critical to overturning the 83% statistic of struggling learners entering city kindergarten classrooms (Welsh et al., 2010). ELNC, formed by Ezeh with seed funding from the W. K. Kellogg Foundation, calculated the education damage from racism, segregation, and poverty. Figureheads saw the correlation between over 80% of children not being prepared for kindergarten and eight in ten vulnerable children not being able to access preschool. These debilitating structural trends had become normative and consistently hampered the future outcomes of children in the community. It was time to be honest about shortcomings of educators in the city and do what needed to be done to break weak achievement cycles. The key to breaking the cycle of poor educational achievement, and its ripple effects, involves access to quality early education and high-quality teachers throughout the K-12 years (Brown, 2010; Darling-Hammond, 2000; Stronge et al., 2011). Ninety percent of a child's brain development takes place in the first five years (Early Brain Development, 2018), making a quality preschool experience necessary for educational success (Duncan et al., 2007).

One must also be honest about a person's skin color and socio-economic background to undercut generational cycles of weak educational performance (Adams & Singh, 1998; Anderson, 2012; Brito & Noble, 2014; Flanagan, 2017; Heckman, 2011; Ndijuye, 2020). The schooling community deserves both the truth of the problem and solutions. Without the truth, one cannot make a difference in the lives of the children. In tandem, there was a need for the tenacity of a fearless leader (Nicholson et al., 2020), and the backing of a strong financial partner, before other stakeholders would pay attention to the truth and the gravity of the learning problems. Concerned partners needed to bring a new mission and vision to the community's approach to early childhood education. ELNC offered a bold but simple vision: working toward a community where all children, regardless of the neighborhood in which they live, can thrive so that they maximize their God-given potential and become self-sufficient adults.

ELNC was established to lead an innovative, community-based collaborative that would expand and sustain high-quality early education programs in the most vulnerable Grand Rapids neighborhoods. The collaborative leverages funds from private and public foundations, as well as from the State of Michigan and federal government, in order to implement their vision (West et al., 2010). To serve the residents of these vulnerable target neighborhoods most effectively, ELNC intentionally partnered with seven trusted neighborhood-based organizations: Baxter Community Center, Hispanic Center of West Michigan, New Hope Baptist Church, South East Community Outreach Ministries (SECOM) Resource Center, Steepletown Neighborhood Services, The Other Way Ministries, and United Methodist Community House. There is overwhelming evidence in the power of community partnerships for strengthening schooling experiences (Comer & Ben-Avie, 2010; McKie et al., 2011; Wilinski, 2017).

Beyond organizational community partners, the ELNC model includes a two-generational approach and considers parental engagement or involvement (Bettencourt et al., 2020; Heng, 2014) and support to be an essential element of a preschool experience for successful transition to kindergarten or primary school (Hoffman et al., 2020; Pears & Kim, 2021). To better prepare parents for this role, parental support and engagement activities are offered at all preschool sites. The ELNC model speaks to the needs of the whole child, which is a foundational principle of ECE (National Association for the Education of Young Children [NAEYC], 2022). Including parents as a core component of the education children receive at ELNC underscores organizational commitment to serving the needs of each child and their families (McWayne & Melzi, 2014). Clearly, parental engagement reinforces that ELNC site activities will be employed at home. In short, such a model ensures that ELNC preschoolers are receiving a quality education beyond preschool walls because of the two-generational approach (McWayne et al., 2013).

An important difference in the ELNC vision is the focus not just on meeting minimum achievement standards but on reaching the full potential of the learner (Bar-On, 2004). At the core of ELNC is a belief that every child deserves the opportunity to grow their gifts to function independently as a member of society.

The ELNC vision advances more than learning to read independently by grade 3 (Chall, 1983). The model is much more expansive and holistic. ELNC aims for all children to lead successful lives that are brought about by enriching early learning experiences that lead them to embrace and recognize their worth and their value (NAEYC, 2022). Accordingly, the ELNC model exists as an anti-deficit model, which stands as a challenge to much education scholarship orthodoxy (NAEYC, 2022). Much educational research and programs have been grounded in false notions that poor Black and Brown children are not performing in the classroom on par with their white counterparts because of genetics or culture (Herrnstein & Murray, 1996; Iruka, 2020). There are decades of educational discourse blaming kids and their parents for their learning predicaments (Delpit, 2012; Ladson-Billings, 1995, 2006, 2018; López et al., 2010; McGee, 2016; Rosiek & Kinslow, 2016; Solomon et al., 2005).

ELNC could not succumb to such racist theories of learning that fail to account for the systemic problems that weaken opportunities to learn (Gándara et al., 2003). ELNC developed as a model that dared to embrace the gifts and strengths of children who are born able to solve their own problems as long as they have the resources to do so (Raynal et al., 2021). To best serve this vulnerable population, ELNC needed to provide access to basic educational tools from the beginning of each child's learning journey as a prerequisite for success *before* such children entered the public school system (Mariano et al., 2019).

The ELNC model has a mission and vision based on a tangible target. The ELNC aims to solve the 83% preparation gap (Noguera, 2012) problem. In reality, more than the 83% under and unprepared rate of learners entering kindergarten drives the mission of the organization. In broad scope:

> ELNC's MISSION
>
> The Early Learning Neighborhood Collaborative will create and provide targeted neighborhood collaborative partners with technical, developmental, and educational support in order to increase the accessibility of early educational resources for vulnerable children through advocacy.

The mission statement of ELNC is multifaceted and therefore demands further analysis.

"Targeted neighborhood collaborative partners"

ELNC opened very strategically by collaborating with neighborhood-based, integrated, culturally competent, trusted organizations (Halpern et al., 2020; Tilhou et al., 2020). ELNC, a new organization, could not get the families of their target neighborhoods to trust them with neighborhood children unless the organizations they *already* trusted were a part of the solution. From the perspective of seasoned early childhood educators like Ezeh, there was no need to start from scratch or take over in areas where others had a solid track record. Working together to strengthen already-existing services by partnering with community agents helped ELNC and their collaborative to achieve collective goals and beyond.

"Technical, developmental, and educational support"

Education in child development theory, in cultural competence, and in the nuts-and-bolts structures that undergird class time with children have to be in place for a teacher to succeed (Essa & Burnham, 2019; Massing & Matheson, 2021). ELNC approached ECE holistically and structurally. Well-educated and experienced teachers of early learning, along with the new organizational curriculum, are necessary to address the needs of historically underserved children, their neighborhoods, and their communities.

"Accessibility of early educational resources"

ECE depends on access to quality classrooms full of pedagogical resources such as teachers with the experience and intellectual knowledge of child development (Khalfaoui et al., 2020). Access is plentiful for those already connected to resources.

Kurt Reppart, then heading The Other Way, a neighborhood family resource on the city's West Side, reveals that the numbers for who in their own service area could even get into a classroom were shocking.

> [There were] 509 vulnerable children in our catchment area, and at the time of the current reality study. Our local Head Start had three preschool classrooms available—so about 50 kids served out of 509 who need it. There were also some for-profit preschools in the area that were very expensive—so that was another.

The Other Way's statistics are indicative of what was happening in vulnerable neighborhoods all around the city, based on Ezeh's work throughout Grand Rapids (Burr, 2021). Even if a parent could pay a large sum for preschool (and with stagnant wages and rising living costs in West Michigan, that was a possibility for fewer and fewer families), their child still had a 53% chance of not even getting into a preschool for simple lack of classroom availability. Families in low-income neighborhoods in Grand Rapids, with limited finances, simply could not get their children into preschool. Eight in ten children could not access the opportunity to get ready for success in school. When only two in ten children have access to a preschool program in neighborhoods with the greatest economic needs, one must address the problem systemically as well as from a justice perspective (Nxumalo & Adair, 2019). These, and other schooling, problems ELNC set out to remedy.

The financing of early learning programs merits additional attention. Taking from the Organization of Economic Cooperation and Development (OECD), All for Child Care (2018) writes,

> As the Organization of Economic Cooperation and Development (OECD) has observed: 'Significant… funding is necessary to support sustainable and equitable early childhood education. Without this, a shortage of good quality programs, unequal access and segregation of children according to income follows. When the main burden of costs falls on parents, children from disadvantaged backgrounds become less represented in Early Childhood Education and Care provision or the quality of provision is inadequate.
> (All for Child Care, 2018)

All for Child Care goes on to state that regular funding will "guarantee access and quality on a fairly equitable basis for all groups." All for Child Care maintains that whether parents have to shoulder the burden of paying for ECE programs depends on whether such programs are "regarded as a public good" or not. While All for Child Care is based in Canada, these ideas are relevant for understanding the ELNC model in the United States with the W. K. Kellogg Foundation financing partner. As will be described below and in subsequent chapters, Kellogg views equitable ECE as a public good because they refused to put financing of education on parents. In fact, Kellogg helped erect ELNC with the premise that there must be multifaceted financial and other kinds of support for children, parents, and families.

Vulnerable children

As previously mentioned, children with the biggest educational need in Grand Rapids are very vulnerable. They are at risk of not achieving their full potential at school and after graduation in part because they are Black or Brown (Burr, 2021). Forbes (Kotkin, 2015) has identified Grand Rapids as the second worst city in America for Black families. Segregation and racism are a reality in American cities, small and large (Greene et al., 2017). Grand Rapids has been no exception to this historical inequity rule – unless the exception is that city's racial realities are even more deeply ingrained than in other cities. As noted in Chapter 1, stark segregation in West Michigan made too easy for well-meaning white people to be completely unaware that the problems of race and racism even exist (DiAngelo, 2018; Oluo, 2019). Moreover, a certain "West Michigan, Grand Rapids Nice" (Waxman, 2022) sensibility kept some people from bringing up "uncomfortable" realities about race in the city, from speaking truthfully without fear of retribution. This fear in a historically "racialized landscape" just further served to exacerbate systemic problems that go unnoticed by those who are privileged enough to be largely directly unaffected because of their white skin (Greene et al., 2017).

By contrast, ELNC was willing to unearth those realities undermining the ability for certain groups of people in the city to live full and meaningful lives. ELNC took action. Stakeholders saw power in vulnerable communities, which led to ELNC's pursuit of community allyship to those on the socio-economic margins of Grand Rapids. The problem has never been about ability; it has always been about access (Gutiérrez, 2011). Targeted ECE can upset the vulnerability that children experience in certain communities at risk (Fordham & Kennedy, 2017). And access remains, in Grand Rapids as elsewhere, a problem of race and poverty (Dalziel et al., 2015).

But there are popular narratives being pushed to the forefront that seek to downplay the racial problems in the city (Waxman, 2022). Vulnerable Black and Brown children needed leaders who would not dismiss how race impacts vulnerable children's lives.

"The narrative around Grand Rapids as being the best place to raise families, and the amount of charity and philanthropy that happens, wasn't reaching everybody," according to Nadia Brigham, former program officer of W. K. Kellogg Foundation and now Principal of Brigham Consulting, LLC, an organization that focuses on racial equity, leadership development, and community engagement for education justice, health equity, and family economic security. Brigham called upon Ezeh to build the answer to the access problem. "We decided to try to figure out if we could bring our strategic framework to Grand Rapids, centered around early childhood," maintains Brigham. Ezeh emerged as the right person with the academic, intellectual, experiential, and cultural knowledge to enact the Kellogg Foundation ECE initiatives.

What set the Kellogg Foundation apart from other stakeholders of the past emanates from their view of ECE as a social justice issue (Stukkie, 2012; W. K. Kellogg Foundation, 2022). And Ezeh has always challenged the status quo, which she learned from her father when she was growing up in Nigeria (Ezeh, 2020). Accordingly, the Kellogg Foundation's mission fully aligned with Ezeh's worldview.

> 'The Kellogg foundation mission is to create the conditions that will propel vulnerable children forward,' notes Brigham. 'We have a value in our foundation in believing in the inherent capacity of communities to solve their own problems. Racial equity and community engagement are approaches that access the DNA of our investors—it's the way we do our work. **ELNC is a critical beacon** around that work. It realizes our mission in those very nuanced and critical ways in that it serves to prepare young children and vulnerable children, within their cultural context, with an eye towards racial equity.'

Brigham states that children of color and voices from communities of color in the area were not being included in conversations about ECE, about what they needed to succeed. Strategy and development work was carried out by white neighbors. Ezeh and Kellogg were a natural relationship waiting to be forged.

Nadia Brigham observes that Kellogg's recognition of Ezeh as the emerging leader of a new model of ECE challenged the status quo.

> Unfortunately, even Dr. Ezeh, the most highly educated person in the field of ECE in the region, could not get a seat at the table with leading stakeholders. Dr. Ezeh traveled around the world giving speeches and consulting, but she was cut off from conversations on ECE in her own city in the United States. As a woman, a Black person, and an immigrant—and someone who refused to play 'West Michigan Nice' to keep everyone comfortable—Dr. Ezeh recognized the barriers undercutting our children's success because she was facing those barriers herself, observes Brigham.

As a result, funding Ezeh to lead ECE initiatives in Grand Rapids proved to be a form of anti-discrimination at the leadership level as much as it did at the learner level.

It was not just Ezeh who was left out of those key conversations. ECE circles in West Michigan managed to systematically exclude all Black and Brown scholars from leadership decision-making. "Then there was no representation on the [Kent County Family and Children Coordinating Council] from those communities," avers Brigham. Brigham and the Kellogg Foundation knew that excluding the communities the Commission was tasked with serving was hurting the outcomes for the community's children. The Kellogg Foundation wanted to do something about the paucity of representation because the Kellogg Foundation wanted results. They needed something more.

The Foundation was aware they had to consult, listen, trust, partner with, and think out of the box.

> 'The first thing we did,' notes Brigham 'was a focus group, consulting with Dr. Ezeh, with the institutions of trust in those communities, both the leaders and the parents, and we

found a whole host of data around what they actually wanted for their children. So then we decided to look at developing a community-based strategy around early childhood, leveraging the cultural assets of the neighborhoods and the institutions that they trusted, for their children'.

Out of that data and those conversations came a collaborative that focused on a place-based, strengths-modeled, multi-generational (empowering parents to own their role as their child's first teacher and advocate), culturally competent belief in children, working to restore access, approaching ECE holistically (Ng & Fisher, 2022).

What happened next showed how these simple changes in approach made all the difference for the children in the program. Of the 228 families served in 2016–2017, according to ELNC:

- Income: 97% of families served made 30k per year or less. Approximately 33%, 76 of those 228 families made *less than $5,000*.
- Race: 6% of families served in ELNC were white.
- Education: Over two-thirds of parents had a high-school diploma or less. Further, 48 out of 228 families had parents who had not completed high school or gotten a GED.
- Readiness: Children entering ELNC did not meet preschool expectations at staggering numbers (The percentage of children ready for school at the onset was just 35% in social–emotional development, 76% in physical development, 43% in cognitive development, 38% in literacy, 47% in language development, and 35% in mathematics).

According to ELNC's annual report for the 2016–2017 academic year, as demonstrated in the ELNC versus the Kent Intermediate School District (KISD) of the Great Start Readiness Program (GSRP) Results chart below, the results were remarkable.

> Kent ISD [KISD] is a local educational service agency devoted to achievement for all students…[serving] the community by helping… schools prepare students to be successful in work and life… Primary customers are the

students, teachers, staff and administrators of 20 public school districts, Christian and Catholic schools and Public School Academies.

(Kent ISD, 2022)

In particular, free schooling is provided to four-year-olds in the Grand Rapids area of Michigan. Through informational exchange between ELNC and district partners and collaborators, evidence has been provided demonstrating learners participating in ELNC programs performed better than learners enrolled in other schools in the area. And, in literacy, learners from ELNC and other area schools "tie." In other words, four-year-olds enrolled in ELNC outperformed four-year-olds from other pre-primary school learning services in the area. Even with economic, racial, and educational barriers for these families, the results for children participating in an ELNC classroom exceeded expectations on the local level. ELNC has also received praise at the state level, thanks to four and five star rated classrooms as per the State of Michigan Quality Preschool Rating Scale (2022). ELNC classrooms were culturally competent and worked to empower parents to reclaim their role in their child's educational development, resulting in the collaborative outpacing any benchmarks (Figure 1.1).

After just five years into the programming, 91% of graduating students from ELNC classrooms are ready for kindergarten,

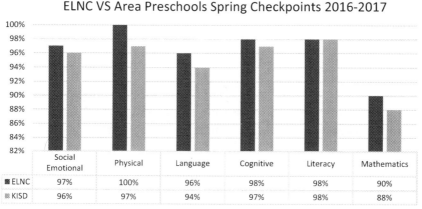

FIGURE 1.1 County wide Preschools NOT KISD

compared to the 17% rate for children prepared for kindergarten in the study highlighted by Grand Rapids Public School's superintendent that preceded the work of ELNC, according to ELNC's (2010–2015) Report Card. As the figure above shows, ELNC students were meeting expectations for development in all areas, not just in educational areas (e.g., 97% for social-emotional development, 100% for physical development, 98% in cognitive development, 98% in literacy, 96% in language, and 90% in mathematics). The new early childhood organization had set a high goal: 75% of their children being assessed as ready for kindergarten. Taking the percentage of those ready to learn from 17% to 75% would have been incredible enough, but the organization far surpassed statistical targets it set, resulting in a 100% kindergarten readiness rate.

The how

How does ELNC create such impressive achievement success rates? So far, evidence shows ELNC had funders with a public good, social justice agenda, and collaborative partnerships with existing community institutions, and ELNC chose a leader with the academic and experiential chops. Another way to succeed is through programming that is more than just class curriculum for preschoolers. Along with collaborative work with institutions of trust in the community, there is a variety of programming led by K'Sandra Earle, Associate Director, that is not just considered ancillary, but in fact an integral part of the structure for a child's positive school readiness.

Parent programs

In line with research (Anthony & Ogg, 2019), ELNC considers parental involvement, engagement, and support to be an essential element of a successful pre-primary experience. To better prepare parents for this role, parent engagement activities are offered at all pre-kindergarten sites:

- ♦ Parent engagement events
- ♦ Parent conferences

- It Starts with Play & Curriculum nights
- Family Coach providing mentoring, resource referrals, and ongoing follow-up
- Family-Centered Social Capital building plan

Teacher development

A focal area for ELNC is the development of teachers of color in part because research so overwhelmingly supports staffing schools with learners of color with teachers of similar racial, ethnic, and cultural backgrounds (Downey & Pribesh, 2004). ELNC teachers are encouraged and supported to achieve their highest potential through various opportunities:

- Individual professional development
- WOW! Fridays (monthly in-service training)
- Teacher mentorship program
- Leadership development series

Partner capacity building

ELNC has spent considerable time expanding partner agencies' capacity through technical assistance.

- Building ELNC culture
- Working as a collaborative
- Cultural competency
- Grassroots advocacy training
- Backoffice support

"Believing in children," "Empowering families," "Collaborating with institutions of trust," and "Valuing the voices of the community served" are all organizational themes that are changing the reality for Grand Rapids area children as ELNC overturns weak and non-existent access to quality early learning so that neighborhood children have a solid foundation for independent adulthood. And ELNC's timeline that includes various milestones is evidence of the quality early childhood educational institution that it has become (Figure 1.2).

2009

- On Saturday, February 21, 2009, Grand Rapids Public Schools (GRPS) Superintendent Dr. Bernard Taylor, Jr. sent a shockwave to the Grand Rapids community in his "State of the Schools" address that "83% of children are not ready for Kindergarten."
- Chana Edmond Verley, Senior Program Officer at the Doug & Maia DeVos Foundation, invited Dr. Nkechy Ekere Ezeh and select community leaders to a study tour of Geoffrey Canada's Harlem Children's Zone – The Baby College in Harlem, New York.
- Dr. Nkechy Ekere Ezeh of PONA Consulting L3C was engaged by W.K. Kellogg Foundation (WKKF) to investigate why Grand Rapids children entering GRPS were not ready for kindergarten.
- Dr. Nkechy Ekere Ezeh conducted a Current Reality Report detailing the demographics of vulnerable neighborhoods in the core city of Grand Rapids that provided some clarity as to the *why*:
    - 25.9% of infants live with incomes below the poverty level.
    - 66.6% of infants have Medicaid-covered birth.
    - 54.9% of infants born have moms without a high-school diploma.
    - 19.4% of infants born have moms who are still in their teens.

FIGURE 1.2 ELNC Milestones 2009–2022.

♦ Perhaps, the most startling statistic was this: *Existing quality, licensed early childhood learning programs for children four and younger had the capacity to serve only 17% of the children.*

2010

♦ Dr. Nkechy Ekere Ezeh was tapped by WKKF to lead a collaborative process with grassroots organizations to plan, design, pilot, and implement "an intentional preschool service system aimed at providing, expanding, and sustaining the capacity of quality early care and education programs in the vulnerable neighborhoods of Grand Rapids." The planning led to a new organization – Early Learning Neighborhood Collaborative (ELNC).

ELNC founding partner organizations and directors are:

- ♦ Baxter Community Center – Program Director, Sharon LaChapelle
- ♦ Hispanic Center of Western Michigan (HCWM) – Chief Executive Officer, Martha Gonzalez Cortes
- ♦ South East Community Outreach Ministries (SECOM) – Executive Director, Kathy Brower
- ♦ Steepletown Neighborhood Services – Executive Director, Dick Bulkowski
- ♦ The Other Way Ministries – Executive Director, Kurt Reppart
- ♦ New Hope Baptist Church – Senior Pastor, Rev. Howard Earle
- ♦ The United Methodist Community House – Executive Director, Richard Clanton

FIGURE 1.2 (Continued).

2011

- Dr. Jim Edwards and Teri Horton from the Non Profit Center at the Dorothy A. Johnson Center for Philanthropy at Grand Valley State University led the partners through the process of development of organizational capacity, infrastructure, and the governance and organizational structure.
- The Doug and Maria DeVos Family Foundation expressed a desire for ELNC to co-lead the development of their new Baby Scholars model with Spectrum Health Strong Beginnings and Arbor Circle. ELNC provided Baby Scholars (a project of Believe to Become) an abbreviated preschool for children ages 3 and 4 years old. Since ELNC was not fully formed, PONA Consulting L3C, under the leadership of Dr. Nkechy Ekere Ezeh, served as the project manager of Baby Scholars during the interim. The first Baby Scholars cohort began in September of 2011.
- ELNC partners began working with Opportunities Exchange to develop a sustainability plan and a business model. With a business model set, we submitted our proposal to the W.K. Kellogg Foundation.
- ELNC received its IRS determination letter of tax-exempt status from the IRS.
- WKKF awarded ELNC a $5 million grant to make Dr. Nkechy Ekere Ezeh vision (ELNC) a reality. WKKF channeled through two external fiduciaries, New Venture Funds and United Way, allowing ELNC to build its own internal capacity.
- Dana Boals became the Founding Board Chair and Celeste Sanchez, the Vice Chair.
- During the first official board meeting, the budget was approved and Dr. Nkechy Ekere Ezeh was appointed as ELNC Founder/Chief Executive Officer.

FIGURE 1.2 (Continued).

- ELNC representatives attended a four-day "Train the Trainer" conference at the Parent Leadership Training Institute where they received the professional development necessary to incorporate parent leaders and increase the voice of the families in ELNC.

2012

- ELNC officially assumed its role as the co-lead of the Baby Scholars program and received its first direct funding from the Doug and Maria DeVos Family Foundation.
- ELNC received an additional $1.5 million over three years to partner with AVANCE Inc. to implement a parent child education program known as PREP (Parent Resource Education and Play Program) for children 0–3 years old.
- ELNC began fatherhood programming (Proud Fathers) at The Other Way Ministries and SECOM Resource Center.
- ELNC received its first corporate donation from OtterBase & Amway One By One.
- While preparing to implement the PREP program, staff also focused on opening culturally relevant preschool classrooms in the fall.
- Knowing that the westside of Grand Rapids had very limited preschool capacity, ELNC leased and began renovations at the vacant Roosevelt Child Development Center from Grand Rapids Public Schools.
- The Parent Leadership Institute started at The Other Way Ministries and PREP started at New Hope Baptist Church.
- ELNC opened its first classrooms, offering high-quality, intentionally designed preschool for 36 children at United Methodist Community House (UMCH) and Baxter Community Center. A third classroom open at Living Stones Academy.

FIGURE 1.2 (Continued).

- Renovation of two more classrooms began at San Juan Diego (Hispanic Center) and SECOM.
- Dr. Nkechy Ekere Ezeh formed the Anchor Organization Network (AON) that included: Grand Rapids Urban League, Grand Rapids African American Health Institute (GRAAHI), Family Outreach Center, Baxter Community Center, and United Methodist Community House (UMCH). This network was formed to serve as a community of practice to design and implement a collaborative model for the purpose of creating a platform for the development and support of Emerging Indigenous Leaders (EIL), thereby cultivating a new generation of leadership and ensuring the sustainability of current initiatives. AON is now Urban Core Collective.

2013

- New ELNC Centers:
    - SECOM opened a new center – Little Steps Preschool.
    - Hispanic Center of West Michigan's La Escuelita Preschool program was opened at San Juan Diego.
    - Steepletown Neighborhood Services opened its preschool program.
    - In partnership with GRPS, ELNC rehabbed the old Roosevelt Preschool building and renamed it Early Learning Center (ELC). Mayor George Heartwell, the ELNC board members, and partners opened the ELC's four classrooms.
    - Mayor George Heartwell led the children in the world's shortest bike parade.
    - ELNC Partners designated ELC as their ELNC model site.

FIGURE 1.2 (Continued).

- The first ELNC Parenting Conference was held with 41 parents in attendance and featured Grand Rapids Public Schools Superintendent, Teresa Weatherall-Neal, as the keynote speaker.
- The Parent Leadership Training Institute (PLTI) also held its first graduation at New Hope Baptist Church with 17 parent graduates.
- ELNC received its first year of state funding for 160 four-year-old Great Start Readiness Program (GSRP) preschool slots.
- One hundred seventy-one students crossed the stage, representing ELNC's first graduating class at UMCH, San Juan Diego (Hispanic Center), Baxter, and SECOM.
- A group of 16 parents also "graduated" by completing the PREP program at New Hope Baptist Church and celebrated their success with a ceremony.
- K'Sandra Earle started as ELNC's Early Childhood Education Director to ensure that each ELNC site meets the quality standards that are held by the agency.

2014

- ELNC piloted center-based infants and toddler program at The Other Way Ministries.
- PONA Consulting L3C, in partnership with ELNC, developed the "Empowering Parents, Impacting Children" (EPIC) model, transitioning ELNC into a two-generation program.
- ELNC partners began a process to build the "ELNC Culture." Dr. Regina McClinton was engaged to assist them in achieving their goals in intercultural competence and inclusion.

FIGURE 1.2 (Continued).

30 ◆ The ELNC model

- ◆ UMCH conducted ELNC's first GSRP Summer Preschool program for 32 children from the West Side neighborhood, helping us deliver early childhood education year-round.
- ◆ Eric Foster from Progressive Strategies was engaged to lead a series of sessions on grassroots advocacy with ELNC parents as part of ELNC Parent leadership. He also provided coaching to Dr. Ezeh on Advocacy and Public Policy.
- ◆ ELNC hosted its first legislative luncheon on the Early Learning Center for three members of the State's House of Representatives: Lisa Posthumus Lyons, Chair of the House Education Committee; Brandon Dillon, who served on House Appropriations Committee for Education; and Rob VerHeulen.

2015

- ◆ ELNC officially added Advocacy to its scope of work. ELNC began the implementation of a State Legislative Advocacy program. Led by Dr. Nkechy Ekere Ezeh, the organization created a profile amongst lawmakers, positioning itself as a leading resource in the field of Early Childhood Education public policy. ELNC became the loudest voice and the only organization in Lansing advocating singularly and purposefully for Early Childhood Education.
ELNC Advocacy Goals:
  - ◆ Michigan Department of Education (MDE) to approve an exemption to its rules on eligible transportation reimbursements. This will make it possible for Community-Based Organization to access their transportation dollars for the purpose of providing

FIGURE 1.2 (Continued).

transportation to the children attending their Great Start Readiness Program (GSRP).
- ♦ Increase the full-day GSRP slot allowance so that it is parity with that of the K-12 foundation grant. This increases the full-day GSRP allowance from $7,250 to $8,111 that ties GSRP per slot funding directly to the K-12 foundation grant so that GSRP funding does not fall behind again in the future.
- ♦ Three-Year Old Pilot Program Funding – ELNC requested funds to evaluate the relative impact, on vulnerable children, of one vs two years of preschool education.

- ♦ ELNC increased the number of children served to 338, meaning 338 chances for a student to receive the early childhood education they desperately need.
- ♦ William Bennett became the second Board Chair.
- ♦ Senator Geoff Hansen, Chair of the Senate Education Appropriations Committee, visited ELNC to learn about our program and progress. Such visits are vital to our cause at ELNC, as collaboration between public, private, and government entities is key to the success of our mission.
- ♦ ELNC was announced the winner of WOOD TV 8s "Connecting with Community" Award.
- ♦ ELNC partnered with KaBOOM! for a playground at ELC.
- ♦ Amway Corporation shut down a plant for a day to send over 200 staff to assist in building ELC Playground.

2016

- ♦ ELNC received second award from W.K. Kellogg Foundation for $5.5 million. Funding came directly to ELNC serving as evidence of ELNC's internal capacity.

FIGURE 1.2 (Continued).

- William Bennett, CEO of Otter Base elected Board Chair of ELNC 2017–2020 – Jackie Nickel becomes Board Chair 2020-present – Amirah Vosburgh becomes Board Chair.
- First Annual Legislative day – Over 35 members of ELNC (parents, board members, partners, and staff) went to the Lansing State Capital to advocate for children. ELNC was able to better understand the goals of our state lawmakers, while those legislators were given the chance to hear our message.
- ELNC got approval for an Early Head Start Childcare Partnership Grant to begin classes in 2017! This opened 88 slots for children between the ages of zero and three years old.
- ELNC won the Grand Rapids Chamber of Commerce 2016 Nonprofit of the Year award.
- ELNC received the West Michigan Hispanic Chamber of Commerce's Nonprofit of the Year award.
- **First major advocacy win** – ELNC Secured three years of direct funding in the amount of $175,000 annually in each of the 2016/2017, 2017/2018, and 2018/2019 state budgets ($525,000 in total) for the purpose of three-year-old pilot program.
- HighScope Educational Research Foundation was engaged by MDE to evaluate the three-year-old pilot program.
- The ELNC Board established Advocacy Committee, contributing $30,000 annually to fund all advocacy work. This set the stage for Annual Legislative day with parents, staff, and board members in Lansing, Michigan.
- K'Sandra Earle was named ELNC Associate Director.
- Kimberly Spencer was named ELNC Director of Programs.
- WOOD TV8 invited ELNC to participate in their daybreak newscast during Art Prize.
- ELNC joined the National Council of La Raza (now UnidosUS). UnidosUS is the nation's largest Latino nonprofit advocacy organization.

FIGURE 1.2 (Continued).

2017

- ELNC Director of Community Engagement, Eva Martinez, started a Community Readers program to invite prominent members of the community to read to children. Eva Aguirre Cooper (WOOD TV8) became our first Community Reader. Over the years, leaders such as former presidents of Grand Valley State University and Grand Rapids Community College, Grand Rapids, Police Chief Eric Winstrom, and Grand Rapids Mayor Rosalynn Bliss among others have read to our preschoolers.
- Second Annual Legislative Day in Lansing to advocate for early childhood education. Close to 40 parents, staff, and board members attended.
- ELNC officially launches Early Head Start programming begins at UMCH and The Other Way Ministries for Infants & Toddlers through the Early Head Start Childcare Partnership Grant.
- ELNC, in partnership with Aquinas College, was awarded $900,000 from the W.K. Kellogg Foundation to address the shortage of qualified teachers of color.
- Dr. Ezeh created and led a six-month "leading while learning" leadership development program as part of her WKKF Fellowship project titled, Grow Your Own Leaders, to increase the number of leaders of color at ELNC.
- ELNC added new service partners through Early Head Start Childcare Partnership Grant:
    - Grand Rapids Community College Preschool Lab
    - YMCA @ Covenant House

FIGURE 1.2 (Continued).

2018

- ELNC Board members (Dana Boals), partners (Richard Clanton & Howard Earle), parents (Shanee Clinton), and staff (Dr. Ezeh and K'Sandra Earle) presented the ELNC Model at Kent County's *Ready by Five* Summit.
- ELNC hosted the "It Starts with Play" community event. It was an opportunity to educate parents about the importance of play.
- Third Annual Legislative Day – ELNC held its second Annual Legislative Day in Lansing to advocate for early childhood education. Bus load of 40 parents, staff, and board members attended.
- The Refugee Education Center joined ELNC as a service partner through our Early Head Start Childcare Partnership Grant.
- Marvin Sapp Ministries (Kingdom Care Early Learning Center) opened an Early Head Start site.
- Second Advocacy win – Michigan Department of Education (MDE) approved an exemption to its rules on eligible transportation reimbursements. With this, it was easier for Community-Based Organizations to access this money for the purpose of providing transportation to the children attending their Great Start Readiness Program (GSRP).
- Steepletown Neighborhood Services opened an Infant & Toddlers classroom through our Early Head Start Childcare Partnership Grant.
- ELNC established a consulting arm – Technical Assistance for Social Change (ELNC TASC) – to assist communities who deserve to work with key stakeholders (community groups, local providers, funders, state agencies, etc.), and who desire to develop place-based solutions that

FIGURE 1.2 (Continued).

- eliminate barriers preventing vulnerable families from accessing quality early learning opportunities.
- Pastor Chris McCoy of New Level Sports Ministries expressed a desire to bring the ELNC Model to Battle Creek.
- WKKF engaged ELNC CEO, Dr. Nkechy Ekere Ezeh to lead a collaborative process to seek solutions to address the critical lack of accessible quality early learning opportunities available for vulnerable children in Battle Creek.
- ELNC received the Grand Rapids Area Black Businesses Collaboration Award.
- The new school year began and we served over 1,800 children to date.
- ELNC begins its REAL Dads program (a revamp of the Proud Fathers program), offering support to fathers.
- ELNC hosts its first annual ICONS Gala at City Flats Hotel.

2019

- Battle Creek partners adopted ELNC's name creating the Early Learning Neighborhood Collaborative-Battle Creek (ELNC-BC)! Jackie Nickel become the third Board Chair.
- ELNC implements a "Reflections" event to showcase our data to the community and get feedback on our work.
- Fourth Annual Legislative Day in Lansing to advocate for early childhood education. Bus load of parents, staff, and board members attended.
- ELNC celebrates ten years of impact!
- ELNC joins Hope Starts Here Detroit and Flint Early Childhood Network in Lansing to advocate for vulnerable children.

FIGURE 1.2 (Continued).

- Dr. Ezeh and her early childhood students at Aquinas College created a documentation panel to commemorate ELNC's ten-year anniversary.
- ELNC program staff moved to a new location on Hall Street to better streamline communication.
- ELNC received the Distinguished Community Trustee Award and Detroit's Corp! Salute to Diversity Award.
- ELNC received $5.4M to take the ELNC Model to Battle Creek ELNC received $5.4M to take the ELNC Model to Battle Creek. as a project of New Level Sports Ministries (NLSM).

  ELNC-Battle Creek founding partner organizations and directors are:
  - Catching the Dream Learning Center – Pastor Biak Thang and Lashi Mai
  - Grace Health – Dr. Peter Chang and Sonja Elder
  - New Level Sports Ministries – Pastor Christopher McCoy and Marcel Heath
  - Sanctuary of Praise – Pastor Harrison LeMon and Hazel LeMon
  - Sugar & Spice Child Care Center – Maude Perry and Myna Austin
- ELNC establishes Early Learning Neighborhood Collaborative-Battle Creek (ELNC-BC) office.
- Pastor Chris McCoy becomes ELNC-BC interim Project Director.
- ELNC adopted the High Scope curriculum.
- The Kalamazoo Community Foundation (KCF) engaged ELNC CEO, Dr. Nkechy Ekere Ezeh to provide technical assistance to Northside Preschools – a network of Black-owned childcare centers on the north side of Kalamazoo. Six months later, ELNC added Latinx-owned and operated childcare centers in east and west Kalamazoo.

FIGURE 1.2 (Continued).

2020

- KCF charged Dr. Ezeh to lead a collaborative process to seek solutions to increase number of quality early learning opportunities available for vulnerable Black and Brown children in Kalamazoo. Amirah Vosburgh elected ELNC 4th Board Chair.
- Kent Intermediate School District awarded ELNC 586 slots this year – an increase of 166 slots – the highest of any community-based organization.
- GLOBAL pandemic (COVID-19) occurred. Programs were virtual, but ELNC Family Coaches were on the ground delivering diapers and food supplies to our families.
- Our Founder and CEO, Dr. Ezeh, published her memoir! NWA ENYI – Child of an Elephant Lessons Learned From My Father, a Nigerian Chief, About Child Development and Affirmation.

2021

- Fifth Annual Legislative Day – Due to the pandemic, ELNC hosted its first ever virtual legislative forum.
- ELNC partnered with IFF, Boston Square Neighborhood Association, and Amplify GR to expand affordable childcare option in the Zipcode 49507 neighborhood.
- ELNC graduations are moved outdoors due to COVID-19.
- Angela Cunningham-Burrows named Director of Communications & Fund Development.

FIGURE 1.2 (Continued).

- ♦ ELNC hosted Governor Whitmer as she unveiled her child care expansion proposal.
- ♦ ELNC was selected as the beneficiary of Ruth's Chris Cares Charity Golf Event.
- ♦ ELNC-Battle Creek officially opened a brand-new early childhood education center – Catching the Dream Learning Center (CDLC). CDLC is the first Burmese-owned and operated early childhood center in the United States. CDLC is a multilingual program.
- ♦ ELNC partnered with Comcast to raise awareness around Internet Essentials (IE) and a new program – Emergency Broadband Benefit (EBB). Comcast donated over 75 chrome books to our families.
- ♦ Third Major Advocacy win – The Governor and Senate raised the per-child full-day slot payment from $7,250 up to the proposed minimum foundation allowance level of $8,275 for the Michigan's free four-year-old preschool program – Great Start Readiness Program (GSRP). In addition, funding was included in the budget to open up an additional 18,000 half day slots for four-year-olds state wide.
- ♦ Governor Gretchen Whitmer returned to see the impact of her childcare expansion and to recognize ELNC's hard work.
- ♦ Stryker Johnson Foundation awards ELNC $12.4M to take ELNC Model to Kalamazoo.

ELNC-Kalamazoo founding partners and director are:

- ♦ El Concilio Kalamazoo – Adrian Vasquez
- ♦ Family Health Center – Denise Crawford
- ♦ JDI Learning Center – Gwendolyn Jennings
- ♦ New Genesis Learning Center – Anquanette Wilbon
- ♦ Preschool International – Isabella Robinson
- ♦ S.E.E.D.S Learning Center – Cathy Wortham
- ♦ YWCA of Kalamazoo – Nichole Blum

FIGURE 1.2 (Continued).

2022

- VOCES of Battle Creek joins ELNC-Battle Creek.
- ELNC establishes Early Learning Neighborhood Collaborative-Kalamazoo (ELNC-KZOO) office.
- ELNC is officially now in three communities in Michigan – Grand Rapids, Battle Creek, and Kalamazoo.
- The expansion into other communities created the urgent need to revise our ELNC organizational structure. The ELNC board underwent a four-month strategic plan for the overall structure of ELNC (corporation).
- The ELNC board voted that expansion, and all programming will be under the umbrella of one 501 (c) (3) organization with all community projects being identified as a project of ELNC. The board also concluded that a central ELNC office will ensure consistent programming and offer administrative efficiencies. The ELNC board will become a with members from our cities of impact and the western Michigan region. The ELNC Board will become a state wide board.
- ELNC-KZOO hired its first staff member, Ms. Britney Lewis. Ms. Lewis serves as the Administrative Manager for ELNC-KZOO providing support to the Kalamazoo office and coordination of office operations and procedures.
- ELNC-BC Catching the Dream Learning Center graduated its first class of 40 preschoolers.
- ELNC Community Readers Program returns with Grand Rapids Mayor Rosalynn Bliss as our guest reader after a two-year hiatus due to COVID-19.
- Annemarie Valdez was selected to fill a newly created position, Chief Impact Officer.
- Shawna Smith selected as ELNC-KZOO Project Director.

FIGURE 1.2 (Continued).

- ELNC establishes its headquarter at 1400 Leonard Street, Grand Rapids, MI 49505. ELNC-Grand Rapids also housed at Leonard Street.
- ELNC welcomed Global Open Learning & Development (GOLD) Preschools as a service partner. GOLD Preschools will implement the first ever International Preschool of the Arts – a Reggio Inspired Program in the core city of Grand Rapids.
- ELNC-BC and Battle Creek Public School partnered to develop strategies to reach children that have not been enrolled in a center-based program or other formal, quality early childhood programs.
- ELNC created "Partnering with Parents in Teaching (PPT)" – a pipeline to childcare worker program in response to the shortage of teachers.

FIGURE 1.2 (Continued).

References

Adams, C., & Singh, K. (1998). Direct and indirect effects of school learning variables on the academic achievement of African American 10th graders. *Journal of Negro Education, 67*(1), 48–66.

All for Child Care. (2018, January 14). *How should early learning and child care be funded in Canada?* Retrieved from https://allforchildcare.ca/2018/01/14/how-should-early-learning-and-child-care-in-canada-be-funded/

Anderson, C. (1994). *Black labor, White wealth : The search for power and economic justice*. Powernomics Corp of Amer.

Anderson, E. (2012). Reflections on the Black-White achievement gap. *Journal of School Psychology, 50*, 593–597.

Anthony, C. J., & Ogg, J. (2019). Parent involvement, approaches to learning, and student achievement: Examining longitudinal mediation. *Journal of School Psychology, 34*(4), 376–385.

Bar-Kochva, I., & Nevo, E. (2019). The relations of early phonological awareness, rapid naming and speed of processing with the development of spelling and reading: A longitudinal examination. *Journal of Research in Reading, 42*(1), 97–122.

Bar-On, A. (2004, February). Early childhood care and education in Africa. *Journal of Early Childhood Research, 2*(1), 67–84. https://doi.org/10.1177/1476718x0421004

Bembry, K. L., Jordan, H. R., Gomez, E., Anderson, M. C., & Mendro, R. L. (1998, April). *Policy implications of long-term teacher effects on student achievement*. Paper presented at the 1998 Annual Meeting of the American Educational Research Association, San Diego, CA.

Bettencourt, A. F., Gross, D., Bower, K., Francis, L., Taylor, K., Singleton, D. L., & Han, H. R. (2020). *Identifying meaningful indicators of parent engagement in early learning for low-income, urban families*. Urban Education.

Bodovski, K., & Youn, M.-J. (2011). The long-term effects of early acquired skills and behaviors on young children's achievement in literacy and mathematics. *Journal of Early Childhood Research, 9*(1), 4–19.

Boyer, E. L., & The Carnegie Foundation for the Advancement of Teaching. (1991, November 1). *Ready to learn: A mandate for the nation (Carnegie Foundation for the Advancement of Teaching)* (1st ed.). Jossey-Bass.

Brito, N. H., & Noble, K. G. (2014). Socioeconomic status and structural brain development. *Frontiers in Neuroscience, 8*, 276.

Brown, C. P. (2010). balancing the readiness equation in early childhood education reform. *Journal of Early Childhood Research, 8*(2), 133–160.

Burr, A. (2021, August 18). *Transforming learning spaces: Program aims to improve access to early childhood education*. Mlive. Retrieved September 26, 2022, from https://www.mlive.com/public-interest/2021/08/transforming-learning-spaces-program-aims-to-improve-access-to-early-childhood-education.html

Center for Educational Performance and Information. (2010). https://www.michigan.gov/cepi

Chall, J. S. (1983). *Stages of reading development*. New York, NY: McGraw-Hill.

Clerkin, A., & Gilligan, K. (2018, March 15). Pre-school numeracy play as a predictor of children's attitudes towards mathematics at age 10. *Journal of Early Childhood Research, 16*(3), 319–334.

Comer, J. P., & Ben-Avie, M. (2010, April 20). Promoting community in early childhood programs: A comparison of two programs. *Early Childhood Education Journal*, *38*(2), 87–94.

Dalziel, K. M., Halliday, D., & Segal, L. (2015, February 17). Assessment of the cost–benefit literature on early childhood education for vulnerable children. *SAGE Open*, *5*(1), https://doi.org/10.1177/2158244015571637

Darling-Hammond, L. (2000). Teacher quality and student achievement: A review of state policy evidence. *Educational Policy Analysis Archive*, *8*(1), 1–44.

Darney, D., Reinke, W. M., Herman, K. C., Stormont, M., Ialongo, N. S. (2013). Children with co-occurring academic and behavior problems in first grade: Distal outcomes in twelfth grade. *Journal of School Psychology*, *51*(1), 117–128.

Davoudzadeh, P., McTernan, M. L., & Grimm, K. J. (2015). Early school readiness predictors of grade retention from kindergarten through eighth grade: A multilevel discrete-time survival analysis approach. *Early Child Research Quarterly*, *32*, 183–192.

Delpit, L. D. (2012). *Multiplication is for white people: Raising expectations for other people's children*. New York, NY: New Press.

DiAngelo, R. (2018). *White fragility: Why it's so hard for White People to talk about racism* (reprint ed.). Boston, MA: Beacon Press.

Downey, D. B., & Pribesh, S. (2004). When Race Matters: teachers' evaluations of students' classroom behavior. Sociology of Education, 77, 267–282. http://dx. doi.org/10.1177/003804070407700401

Duncan, G. J., Dowsett, C. J., Claessens, A., Magnuson, K., Huston, A. C., Klebanov, P., & Japel, C. (2007). School readiness and later achievement. *Developmental Psychology*, *43*, 1428–1445.

Early Brain Development. (2018, May 11). *The science of early learning*. Retrieved September 24, 2022, from https://thescienceofearlylearning.com/science/early-brain-development/

ELNC. (2010–2015). Report Card.

Essa, E. L., & Burnham, M. M. (2019). *Introduction to early childhood education* (8th ed.). New York, NY: Sage Publications.

Ezeh, N. (2020). *Nwaenyi: Child of an elephant: Lessons learned from my father, a Nigerian Chief, about child development and affirmations*. Independently published.

Feinstein, L., Engel, M., Brooks-Gunn, J., Sexton, H., Duckworth, K., & Japel, C. (2007). School readiness and later achievement. *Developmental Psychology, 43*, 1428–1446.

Flanagan, C. (2017). The time is now: Empowering educators to examine and address race in their classrooms. *Journal of Museum Education, 42*(1), 22–31.

Fordham, L., & Kennedy, A. (2017, December). Engaging vulnerable children and families: Learning from a new model of education and care. *Australasian Journal of Early Childhood, 42*(4), 30–37.

Freire, P., & Macedo, D. (1987, July 31). *Literacy: Reading the word and the world* (0 ed.). Westport, CT: Praeger.

Fuson, K. C., Clements, D. H., & Sarama, J. (2015, October 26). Making early math education work for all children. *Phi Delta Kappan, 97*(3), 63–68.

Gándara, P., Rumberger, R., Maxwell-Jolly, J., & Callahan, R. (2003). English learners in California schools: Unequal resources, unequal outcomes. *Educational Policy Analysis Archives, 11*(36), 1–52.

Giroux, H. A. (2001, September 30). *Theory and resistance in education: Towards a pedagogy for the opposition*. Westport, CT: Praeger Publishers.

Greene, S., Turner, M. A., & Gourevitch, R. (2017, August). *Racial residential segregation and neighborhood disparities*. Washington, DC: Mobility Poverty.

Gutiérrez, K. D. (2011). Teaching toward possibility: Building cultural supports for robust learning. *PowerPlay: A Journal of Educational Justice, 3*(1), 22–37.

Halpern, C., Szecsi, T., & Mak, V. (2020, August 18). "Everyone can be a leader": Early childhood education leadership in a center serving culturally and linguistically diverse children and families. *Early Childhood Education Journal, 49*(4), 669–679.

Heckman, J. (2011). The economics of inequality: The value of early childhood education. *American Educator, 35*, 31–47.

Heng, T. T. (2014, March 28). The nature of interactions between Chinese immigrant families and preschool staff: How culture, class, and methodology matter. *Journal of Early Childhood Research, 12*(2), 111–127.

Herrnstein, R. J., & Murray, C. (1996, January 10). *The bell curve: Intelligence and class structure in American life* (A Free Press Paperbacks Book, Illustrated). New York, NY: Free Press.

Hoffman, J. A., Uretsky, M. C., Patterson, L. B., & Green, B. L. (2020). Effects of a school readiness intervention on family engagement during the Kindergarten transition. *Early Childhood Research Quarterly*, *53*, 86–96. https://doi.org/10.1016/j.ecresq.2020.02.005

hooks, b. (1994). *Teaching to transgress*. Oxfordshire: Routledge.

Invernizzi, M., Justice, L., Landrum, T. J., & Booker, K. (2004). Early literacy screening in Kindergarten: Widespread implementation in Virginia. *Journal of Literacy Research*, *36*(4), 479–500.

Iruka, I. U. (2020). Using a social determinants of early learning framework to eliminate educational disparities and opportunity gaps. In Foundation for Child Development (Ed.), *Getting it right: Using implementation research to improve outcomes in early care and education* (pp. 63–86). New York, NY: Foundation for Child Development.

Keesey, S., Konrad, M., & Joseph, L. M. (2014, August 7). Word boxes improve phonemic awareness, letter–sound correspondences, and spelling skills of at-risk kindergartners. *Remedial and Special Education*, *36*(3), 167–180.

Kent ISD. (2022). *Kent ISD*. Retrieved October 15, 2022, from https://www.kentisd.org

Khalfaoui, A., García-Carrión, R., & Villardón-Gallego, L. (2020, March 16). A systematic review of the literature on aspects affecting positive classroom climate in multicultural early childhood education. *Early Childhood Education Journal*, *49*(1), 71–81.

Kotkin, J. (2015, January 15). *The cities where African-Americans are doing the best economically*. Forbes. Retrieved September 26, 2022, from https://www.forbes.com/sites/joelkotkin/2015/01/15/the-cities-where-african-americans-are-doing-the-best-economically/?sh=674494b0164f

Kozol, J. (2006). *The shame of the nation: The restoration of apartheid schooling in America* (reprint ed.). New York, NY: Crown.

Ladson-Billings, G. (1995). Toward a theory of culturally relevant pedagogy. *American Educational Research Journal*, *32*(3), 465–491.

Ladson-Billings, G. (2006). Yes, but how do we do it? Practicing culturally relevant pedagogy. In J. Landsman & C. W. Lewis (Eds.), *White teachers/diverse classrooms: A guide to building inclusive schools, promoting high expectations, and eliminating racism* (pp. 29–42). Sterling, VA: Stylus.

Ladson-Billings, G. (2018). The social funding of race: The role of schooling. *Peabody Journal of Education, 93*(1), 90–105.

Leong, C. K., & Haines, C. F. (1978). Beginning readers' analysis of words and sentences. *Journal of Reading Behavior, 10*(4), 393–407.

López, A., Correa-Chávez, M., Rogoff, B., & Gutiérrez, K. (2010). Attention to instruction directed to another by U.S. Mexican-heritage children of varying cultural backgrounds. *Developmental Psychology, 46*(3), 593–601.

Macmillan, A. (2009). *Numeracy in early childhood: Shared contexts for teaching and learning.* Victoria: Oxford University Press.

Mariano, M., Santos-Junior, A., Lima, J. L., Perisinotto, J., Brandão, C., Surkan, P. J., & Martins, S. S. (2019, December 26). Ready for school? A systematic review of school readiness and later achievement. *Global Journal of Human-Social Science, 19,* 57–71.

Massing, C., & Matheson, M. L. (2021, July 6). *Introduction to early childhood education and care: An intercultural perspective.* Edmonton: Brush Education.

McGee, E. O. (2016). Devalued Black and Latino racial identities: A by-product of STEM college culture? *American Educational Research Journal, 53*(6), 1626–1662.

McKie, B. K., Manswell Butty, J. A., & Green, R. D. (2011, November 2). Reading, reasoning, and literacy: Strategies for early childhood education from the analysis of classroom observations. *Early Childhood Education Journal, 40*(1), 55–61. https://doi.org/10.1007/s10643-011-0489-2

McLaren, P. (2022, September 25). *Life in schools: An introduction to critical pedagogy in the foundations of education* (5th ed.). Hoboken, NJ: Prentice Hall.

McWayne, C., Melzi, G., Schick, A. R., Kennedy, J. L., & Mundt, K. (2013). Defining family engagement among Latino Head Start parents: A mixed-methods measurement development study. *Early Childhood Research Quarterly, 28,* 593–607.

McWayne, C. M., & Melzi, G. (2014). Validation of a culture-contextualized measure of family engagement in the early learning of low-income Latino children. *Journal of Family Psychology, 28*(2), 260.

Melhuish, E., & Gardiner, J. (2019). Structural factors and policy change as related to the quality of early childhood education and care for 3–4 year olds in the UK. *Frontiers in Education, 4*, 35.

Melvin, S. A., Bromer, J., Iruka, I. U., Hallam, R., & Hustedt, J. (2022). *A transformative vision for the authentic inclusion of family child care in mixed-delivery PreK systems*. Chicago, IL: Erikson Institute.

Moore, E. A., Harris, F., Laurens, K. R., Green, M. J., Brinkman, S., Lenroot, R. K., & Carr, V. J. (2014). Birth outcomes and academic achievement in childhood: A population record linkage study. *Journal of Early Childhood Research, 12*(3), 234–250.

Munoz, M. A., & Chang, F. C. (2007). The elusive relationship between teacher characteristics and student academic growth: A longitudinal multilevel model for change. *Journal of Personnel Evaluation in Education, 20*, 147–164.

National Association for the Education of Young Children. (2022). *Principles of child development and learning and implications that inform practice*. Retrieved October 15, 2022, from https://www.naeyc.org/resources/position-statements/dap/principles

Ndijuye, L. G. (2020). The role of home learning environments and socio-economic status in children's learning in Tanzania: A comparison study of naturalized refugee, rural majority, and urban majority population groups. *Journal of Early Childhood Research, 18*(4), 354–370.

Ng, D. T. K., & Fisher, J. W. (2022, April 22). Kindergarten teachers' spiritual well-being impacts holistic early childhood education. *International Journal of Children's Spirituality, 27*(3–4), 1–17.

Nicholson, J., Kuhl, K., Maniates, H., Lin, B., & Bonetti, S. (2020). A review of the literature on leadership in early childhood: Examining epistemological foundations and considerations of social justice. *Early Child Development and Care, 190*(2), 91–122.

Noddings, N. (2005, May 27). *The challenge to care in schools: An alternative approach to education* (2nd ed.). Advances in Contemporary Educational Thought Series. New York, NY: Teachers College Press.

Noguera, P. A. (2003). *City schools and the American dream: Reclaiming the promise of public education* (reprint ed.). Multicultural Education Series. New York, NY: Teachers College Press.

Noguera, P. (2012). The achievement gap and the schools we need: Creating the conditions where race and class no longer predict student achievement. Retrieved from https://journals.sagepub.com/doi/10.3102/0013189X09357621

Nxumalo, F., & Adair, J. K. (2019). Social justice and equity in early childhood education. In C. P. Brown, M. McMullen, & N. File (Eds.), *Handbook of early childhood care and education* (pp. 661–682). Hoboken, NJ: Wiley Blackwell Publishing.

Oluo, I. (2019). *So you want to talk about race* (reprint ed.). Cypress, CA: Seal Press.

Pears, K. C., & Kim, H. (2021). *A two-generational approach to promoting a successful transition to kindergarten* (pp. 322–340). New York, NY: Hindawi.

Raynal, A., Lavigne, H., Goldstein, M., & Gutierrez, J. (2021, May 30). Starting with parents: Investigating a multi-generational, media-enhanced approach to support informal science learning for young children. *Early Childhood Education Journal, 50*(5), 879–889.

Rosiek, J., & Kinslow, K. (2016). *Resegregation as curriculum: The meaning of new racial segregation in U.S. public schools*. New York: Routledge.

Shannon, P. (2014, March 17). *Reading poverty in America* (1st ed.). Abingdon; New York, NY: Routledge.

Slot, P. (2018). *Structural characteristics and process quality in early childhood education and care: A literature review* (OECD Education Working Papers No. 176; OECD Education Working Papers, Vol. 176). Utrecht: Utrecht University.

Smith, N., & Glass, W. (2019). Ready or not? Teachers' perceptions of young children's school readiness. *Journal of Early Childhood Research, 17*(4), 329–346.

Solomon, R. P., Portelli, J. P., Daniel, B. J., & Campbell, A. (2005). The discourse of denial: How White teacher candidates construct race, racism and "White privilege." *Race, Ethnicity, and Education, 8*(2), 147–169.

Stronge, J. H., Ward, T. J., & Grant, L. W. (2011). What makes good teachers good? A cross-case analysis of the connection between teacher effectiveness and student achievement. *Journal of Teacher Education, 62*(4), 339–355.

Stukkie, H. (2012). Early learning neighborhood collaborative prepares children for kindergarten and life. *Rapid Growth*. Retrieved October 15, 2022, from https://www.rapidgrowthmedia.com/features/11082012early.aspx

Swick, K. J., Da Ros, D. A., & Kovach, B. A. (2001). Empowering parents and families through a caring inquiry approach. *Early Childhood Education Journal*, *29*, 65–71.

ten Braak, D., Lenes, R., Purpura, D. J., Schmitt, S. A., & Størksen, I. (2022, February). Why do early mathematics skills predict later mathematics and reading achievement? The role of executive function. *Journal of Experimental Child Psychology*, *214*, 105306.

Tilhou, R., Eckhoff, A., & Rose, B. (2020, March 21). A collective impact organization for early childhood: Increasing access to quality care by uniting community sectors. *Early Childhood Education Journal*, *49*(1), 111–123.

Watts, T. W., Duncan, G. J., Siegler, R. S., & Davis-Kean, P. E. (2014). What's past is prologue: Relations between early mathematics knowledge and high school achievement. *Educational Researcher*, *43*(7), 352–360.

Waxman, O. B. (2022, April 18). Behind "grand rapids nice," police problems run deep in Michigan. *Time*. Retrieved September 27, 2022, from https://time.com/6167659/grand-rapids-race-history/

Welsh, J. A., Nix, R. L., Blair, C., Bierman, K. L., & Nelson, K. E. (2010). The development of cognitive skills and gains in academic school readiness for children from low-income families. *Journal of Educational Psychology*, *102*(1), 43–53.

West, A., Roberts, J., & Noden, P. (2010). Funding early years education and care: Can A mixed economy of providers deliver universal high quality provision? *British Journal of Educational Studies*, *58*(2), 155–179.

Wilinski, B. (2017). *When pre-K comes to school: Policy, partnerships, and the early childhood education workforce*. New York, NY: Teachers College Press.

W. K. Kellogg Foundation. (2022). *The early learning neighborhood collaborative expands its reach to children in underserved communities*. Retrieved September 27, 2022, from https://www.wkkf.org/what-we-do/featured-work/the-early-learning-neighborhood-collaborative-expands-its-reach

2
Leadership

For certain, Ezeh's own experiences and values are embedded directly into the Early Learning Neighborhood Collaborative (ELNC)'s approach to early childhood education (ECE). These include tenacity, belief in your own worth, pouring into our children, empowerment, and place based cultural competency.

Tenacity. Dr. Nkechy Ekere Ezeh is tenacious. This is the word that most comes to mind when describing her personal and professional character.

Ezeh grew up in Nigeria and immigrated to the United States as a young woman. Ezeh's parents provided a foundation for her tenacity by pouring their love into child of an elephant, or the daughter of a chief who always remembered to hear the voices of everyone person in the village - big and small. (Ezeh, 2020). They reminded her of her *worth* as a girl, that she was *important* to the family and village, that she was *capable* of achieving at the highest levels of society. These gifts of affirmation from Ezeh's parents prepared her to face the many obstacles in her way as an immigrant, as a woman, and as a person of color in the United States. The earliest years of her life in which her parents instilled discipline and motivation to work hard made it possible for Ezeh to push past the barriers of a different society that sought to undermine Ezeh's advancement (National Association for the Advancement of Colored People, 2022) and work settings that are designed to marginalize (Jean-Marie et al., 2016). The love and care of her father and mother provided the drive for her to obtain a terminal degree in the field of ECE, and to become a go-to expert of early learning in the Michigan region.

Ezeh brings her own personal experiences – values she learned as a child, as a new immigrant outsider, and mother – as well as her professional aptitude to tend to the children she serves in the Midwest of the United States and beyond. She is determined. Ezeh advocates for what she believes in. Ezeh is willing to walk into spaces in which others tiptoe. She is fully aware of the consequences of being anti-status quo. Luckily, there are many in the Grand Rapids, Michigan, community who admire Ezeh's steadfast voice, championing quality education for the vulnerable. "We have a visionary leader who is aggressive and bold and doesn't take no for an answer," says Kurt Reppart, former Executive Director of The Other Way Ministries and now A city Commissioner. "It [ELNC programming] really wouldn't happen [successfully] without that [sort of leadership aggressiveness]." This bold attitude may have caused some problems in the past in leadership circles in Grand Rapids and beyond, according to Reppart and others who partner with ELNC. Systems, after all, are well established and prefer people who go along without challenging systems, even if people think the systems are wrong (Ramosaj & Berisha, 2014). But Reppart observes that Ezeh has been playing the long game because the future of the children in her community is her priority. The strength of Ezeh as an agitator, too often seen as weakness, was recognized as a necessary tool for success in her work at the ELNC.

Erecting an institution such as the ELNC requires leadership with a tenacious, agitating spirit and people skills. It takes someone who knows that they will hit walls over which few are willing to climb. Leading the ELNC means following logic that not everyone will understand; it means questioning systems in which many have unwavering, dogmatic belief; ELNC is a new system, which takes from and challenges educational orthodoxy. Lorri Santamaria and Andrés Santamaria (2016) describe a sort of leadership that recalls Ezeh's leadership approach to which all should aspire:

> …educational leadership practice can make or break a school. This being the case, it should at the very least include acts or processes that introduce new ideas or

methods, therefore making the educational experience better for all involved. In other words, the leadership should be innovative in nature. Educational leadership should also be responsive enough to change with socio-historical contexts and circumstances to reflect the best knowledge about what works in as many educational configurations as possible. In keeping with demographic shifts and complexities amongst populations in the United States (US) and similar countries contributing to increased levels of cultural, ethnic, and linguistic diversity, leadership practices should be culturally sustaining. As such, these practices should push the boundaries of the status quo leadership practice and further develop existing culturally responsive practices in education so these ways of leading begin to rely upon, support, and reflect local, regional, and global contexts. A shift in leadership in this direction would certainly be a new idea and method, and as a result, signal innovation.

(p. 1)

Based on the theory of culturally sustaining leadership, ELNC must employ leaders who adhere to local demography, culture, and language. The innovation of ELNC can be understood in part by acknowledging historical racial inequities in Grand Rapids (Jelks, 2006) and beyond and actively working to uproot them. Therefore, leading ELNC requires taking an approach that contradicts – sometimes even condemns – the system with which others have become comfortable.

For a scholar like Ezeh, innovative, dissent leadership comes second nature, given previous hardship and upbringing. "My journey to ELNC wasn't an easy journey," admits Ezeh. "There was major pushback all over." "No one wanted to upset our regional leadership norms," Ezeh observed. Reorganizing the system via ELNC so that poor people who may be Black or Brown had equal access to quality ECE was difficult. But, according to Ezeh, that is exactly why she pushed forward. "That's what motivates me with this work," she explains. "Being a minority person, having an accent—people didn't think I knew what I was doing. They didn't believe in me initially." Unfortunately, various international women leaders' experience parallels those of Ezeh (Watson & Normore, 2016). ECE leadership should be equitable at all levels, but Ezeh's testimony reveals that her rise to the top remains nonnormative. Still, the experience of encountering various naysayers, though arduous, prepared Ezeh for the long fight ahead. She was able to marshal strength for Grand Rapids's children. "I understand our children: they're vulnerable, they're poor, their parents don't have a good education," she avers. "So people think, 'why waste time on them?'" But the fight for the vulnerable – that unwillingness to give in and let the status quo win, to let power win the fight again – does not go unnoticed.

Ezeh's fight is grounded in research, which shows that low-income children attending formal ECE increase their chances of enrolling in higher education many years down the road (Garon-Carrier et al., 2022). ECE at minimum prepares learners for kindergarten and primary education (Brown, 2010; Davoudzadeh et al., 2015; Duncan et al., 2007; Kay, 2022; Mariano et al., 2019; Ready at Five, 2020; Smith & Glass, 2019; Welsh et al., 2010) and at maximum for K-16 education and beyond. Based on her own journey, along with what the research says, looking the other way when people are suffering, particularly when there are viable solutions to such suffering, is not a value Ezeh holds. Her parents did not model such a line of behavior for her in Nigeria (Ezeh, 2020). The village takes care of each other.

As the Santamaria and Santamaria quote above shows, one of the reasons why ELNC has had success in ECE with children historically marginalized in the Grand Rapids community has to do with Ezeh's culturalist approach to educational leadership. Ezeh uses culture as the unit of analysis. "Nkechy is a powerful leader," says Dana Boals, founding Board Chair. "She has a way of approaching things from a distinctly cultural lens that is often missing for the families they serve. I am always impressed with her approach. She's doing *with* instead of doing *for*." In other words, this culture-centric approach, working *with* parents and understanding their role as their child's first teacher was modeled to Ezeh by her parents and throughout village life (Ezeh, 2020). Her own cultural worldview demands viewing parents as the true expert on their own child's development. Employing culture as the prism through which to identify early learning problems and how to solve them can perhaps only come from someone who knows the role of parents in education.

Using culture to tend to the needs of children reflects an educational approach to an education problem. Shirley Brice Heath (1982) signaled to the education field that studying preschoolers' home literacy practices with their parents and family members revealed much of what educators needed to know about how children learn at school. Gloria Ladson-Billings (1995) shook the education field nearly 30 years ago with her landmark research theorizing how one teaches best with Black kids. Aria Razfar and Kris Gutiérrez (2003) cataloged the sociocultural shift in ECE research, noting how the field moved away from behavioral and then cognitive psychology in part as a result of Lyndon Johnson's "War on Poverty." The now well-known United States federally funded Project Headstart, which aimed to attack poverty with ECE, began a trajectory that morphed into looking at early learning in homes and at school. The problem with Headstart, Razfar and Gutiérrez maintain, is that "Although Project Head start illustrated the importance of home literacy practices prior to formal schooling, it was limited in that it did not address the unique factors affecting linguistic and racial minority students" (p. 37). Moreover, according to Razfar and Gutiérrez, Headstart's founding premise was based on deficit views of poor Black and Brown preschoolers' achievement. It took a number of education scholars and leaders, many of whom are Black and Brown themselves, to challenge dominant deficit theories of Black and Brown learners and learning that occur across the pre-K-12 spectrum (Davy, 2016; Iruka, 2020; Khalifa, 2018; Lopez, 2016; Scanlan & López, 2014; Shields, 2010; Terrell et al., 2018).

With her expertise in ECE and her own personal experiences, Ezeh contributes intellectually and politically to the anti-deficit conversation. Ezeh knows – deeply and personally – what it means to be underestimated, to be passed by, and to be expected to fail. "This goes back to when she was a young mother in and recent immigrant to the Grand Rapids area and had to figure out what to do to get her children the services she wanted," acknowledges Boals. "She's so invested in what she believes: she knows it can make a difference in lives." Ezeh refused to give up – on her own capabilities and on a community not paying attention to some of its own children. And the reason for the anti-defeatist attitude stems from, besides her upbringing in Nigeria, being a mother herself. Ezeh advocates for other people's children the way she advocated for her own children. Immigrant mothers, like non-immigrant mothers, want what is best for their children (Lee et al., 2018). "It's like the same push I had with my own children: we're going to show them that you can do it," Ezeh admits.

> Anyone else doing this in their community will need someone passionate, someone who is going to take it personal. It's not just a job. Your leader needs to have a chip on their shoulder, a need to prove that your children are capable. That pushes you to go above and beyond.

While some great leaders may not possess similar experiences to those of their constituents, many great leaders do (Meskil, 2016). Educating a child without parental involvement just will not work (Bettencourt et al., 2020), particularly from the perspective of someone who has raised children. Because failure was not an option for raising her own children, Ezeh does not see failure as an option to help educate other people's children.

Belief in your own worth.
Pouring into our children.
Empowerment.
Place-based and culturally competent.

Besides tenacity mentioned above, these are values that circle back to Ezeh's childhood. These values are embedded into her personality and serve as an integral part of her professional life. Ezeh maintains that these values have energized her; they prepared her for the hard work ahead. These values allowed her to believe in herself as a member of her native village in Nigeria as well as in her adopted village of Grand Rapids, MI.

From Africa to North America, Ezeh has enacted these values to help her community's children, culminating in leading ELNC. Jennifer Jones-Morales and Alison M. Konrad (2018) observe that one's propensity to become an "elite" leader centers on early life messages from parents and other adult figures. Talent recognition and encouragement to lead tend to actually start years before leaders take up formal leadership positions. According to Jones-Morales and Alison, would-be leaders develop "relational capital" that results longitudinally in leadership status. Ezeh factoring in how her parents raised her in Nigeria to her leadership success in the United States has social scientific support.

If you ask Ezeh, a tenacious leader, to identify the values given to her by her parents, she will tell you that there are too many to narrow down. The organizational values listed above come from a collection of values Ezeh has accumulated over her lifetime as a little girl of a chief to a grown woman with a doctorate in ECE. Beyond those listed above, consider the following:

Be yourself.
You are unique for a reason.
Find your own path.
Use your skills to do something good.
Show up.
Be proud of yourself.
Whatever you do, put your all in it and do it to the fullest.

What is clear is that tenacity is the root for this list of values. Being tenacious leads one down this value path that is commensurate with ELNC programming. Such values cross-list with those certain traits and skills identified in the field of ECE leadership (Grantham-Caston & DiCarlo, 2021). For instance, tenacity is a form of persistence, which helps to run a business and motivate staff.

A leader in the work of ECE needs drive, passion, and energy, although some Black leaders of ECE centers may downplay these character traits because of negative perceptions (Meskil, 2016). Notwithstanding, according to Rose Simmons, former Director of Programs at United Methodist Community House and ELNC

Partner Advisory Committee Co-Chair, Ezeh uses the right ingredients to carry out ECE initiatives. "Her drive took her to where the possibilities lie," Simmons relays. "You have to have a strong leader. If it's not founded on a passionate, strong leader—and a person who dares, you won't find success." Simmons's declaration suggests that successful ELNC leadership begins with leaders with certain character traits. One must be intrinsically motivated based on one's internal value system to engage in the day-to-day advocacy for children who have historically had few advocates (Grantham-Caston & DiCarlo, 2021). Considering that the sole incentive to work with and for poor kids who come from families with little to no education is simply a moral incentive, one must be determined (Halpern et al., 2020). Early childhood leaders must have sincere belief that devoting energy to causes that require grind and grit with the potential for no reward other than knowing it is right thing to do is a worthy vocational direction about which one must have passion (Douglass, 2017).

A strong leader in ECE cannot just be passionate about education, though, Simmons opines. Such a leader has to also be passionate about righting injustice for *all* of our children (Halpern et al., 2020; Nicholson, 2017). "Ezeh doesn't like to see injustice. An injustice for her is like a death," notes Simmons. "Because of her drive to see justice, especially for African-American kids: that is why we are where we are today." Ostensibly then ELNC is a collaborative for justice. The architecture of the organization is based on making early learning equitable and just, to be consistent with national ECE standards (National Association for the Education of Young Children, 2020) and Ezeh's personal values. ELNC success centers on tenacity *and* justice.

Leading while learning

Practicing a "lead while learning" mantra has reinforced ELNC's success. Such practice cannot be surprising in ECE leadership circles where quality leadership demands lifelong learning (Grantham-Caston & DiCarlo, 2021). In fact, what one hears most often after a mention of Dr. Nkechy Ekere Ezeh's tenacity is this willingness to do the work "beforehand." Ezeh's philosophy is to just start, and the full roadmap will develop along the way. In other words: "We were building the plane while it was flying, and sometimes fixing it in the air." This analogy is commonly used to explain the start of ELNC. There was – and still is – an attitude within the staff and collaborative partners to keep adjusting, to keep learning and growing. Trying new things, and letting go of what's not working, was and is the standard approach. Much like a startup company, ELNC was able to be successful because it was willing to, as the startup world says, "iterate, iterate, iterate." To "iterate" is to try something out, to create a product or service, and then to measure, to get feedback, and quickly adjust accordingly. In the lean startup world, that cycle of product development, of iteration, happens very quickly.

There is a willingness, from a startup perspective, to take everything known – skills, talents, and education – and take a leap of faith, try something new. Equally important, a startup must be willing to pay attention to business results or outcomes, conduct evaluation of its business strategy (Kagan & Hallmark, 2001), and fix what's not working. As the entrepreneurs say, "fail fast."

ELNC has adopted an entrepreneurial approach (Simarasl et al., 2022) – much different than a typical academic or organizational model. The implications have led to ELNC's rapid and notable success where other, comparable institutions could not seem to progress. This sort of entrepreneurship cultivates a sort of leading while learning because of the foundational structure of ELNC. And one example of ELNC's "lead while learning" method was in its staffing. "Originally thought we'd have an executive director and a part-time administrative assistant for that person. So we thought we could do very lean staff—but it just wasn't realistic. We did not want to set ourselves up to fail," admits Melita Powell, former Program Manager at The Other Way Ministries and ELNC Partner Advisory Council Co-Chair. "We continue to think things through differently, and adjust what we need for staff, just like any growing organization," states Powell. An undergirding philosophy is being people rich. ELNC has to be people centric to be taken seriously. The organization professes developing people, albeit people in the earliest stages of the lives. Logically, ELNC should demonstrate via its business model a philosophy that people are essential for collaborative ECE efforts.

As mentioned in Chapter 1, collaboration is key. However, collaboration has its challenges for organizations such as ELNC.

> One of the challenges for anyone thinking about doing this [work] is that a collaborative partner has got all of their own work on their own. So they're looking at this leadership person, this visionary who's convened them and called them together, Powell declares.

What ELNC quickly learned is that collaborative partners are often already understaffed themselves, which is not an uncommon phenomenon in the nonprofit world (Escobar et al, 2021). As a result, organizations such as ELNC simply could not sustain their social justice equity work without administrative staff of their own. However, collaborating with other institutions does not mean one does not have to pull one's own weight. ELNC needs to stand solid, which requires a certain level of interior human resources to function independently. Like just about any independent organization, ELNC cannot rely on community partners to carry out basic day-to-day operations. Collaboration with community partners is for ancillary support to the ELNC mission.

Besides staffing, programming levels were another element that needed to shift significantly with collaborative partnerships. The ELNC plan was to start with adding a single classroom to two partners sites in the first year. "We had it all plotted out and laid out for healthy, slow, sustainable growth: we were going to put another classroom at two sites that were already doing early childhood. That's it," claims Powell. But time-sensitive opportunities arose that forced ELNC to rethink their slow growth plan. In the first year, along with adding classrooms to those two sites, ELNC added a classroom to a third site that has not been used for childcare at all. Moreover, ELNC opened a new building with four classrooms.

ELNC had to accelerate, as opposed to decelerate, growth plans. According to Melita Powell "tabulating growth reveals a total of seven (7) classrooms, as compared to the two (2) originally planned." Moreover, "we went from zero to 150 in 20 seconds," reveals Powell. Sizable shifts like this one requires a willingness to adjust and rework in situ to continually flex with new plans. One must clarify that leading while learning, from an ELNC perspective, centers on having an organizational roadmap. It centers on good planning, to have some direction. However, leading while learning means not only the willingness to change plans on the fly but in fact to expect immediate change of plans based on new information, circumstances, resources, and more (Douglass, 2017; Hujala, 2019). No doubt, the rise and success of ELNC speaks to actual leading while learning.

Leading while learning in an ELNC era speaks to adjusting to all sorts of unexpected problems, roadblocks, and disappointments. For instance, some early parent programs just were not getting the response that the collaborative expected. "So then hard decisions have to be made: if it's not working the way that we thought it would or the way we wanted it to, do we continue it? Do we modify it? Or do we just walk away?" questions Powell. The ELNC team also knew that to get the answers to those questions required listening to the people that education stakeholders may not usually consult: the parents. Racism and classism tend to undercut leadership that includes the voices of parents in program development and other executive leadership decisions (Meskil, 2016).

Leadership learning often begins this way. Part of learning while leading at ELNC entailed growing the capacity for helping parents to learn how to use their own voices and be advocates for their children (Kagan & Hallmark, 2001). This sort of leadership is inherently going against the grain because parents of children at ELNC are used to being overlooked and underestimated for their insight into their children's education and the education for parents themselves. So, advocacy training and empowerment were set into place so that parents would be able to voice what was not working for their children (and what *was* working). The ELNC model developed to include parents as the central, key partner whose voices had to be regularly amplified and heard to carry out the organizational mission (Bettencourt et al., 2020; Halpern et al., 2020; Jacobson & Notman, 2018).

For ELNC operations to reflect an equity mission for poor Black and Brown children, even the organizational chart had to indicate resistance to a societal hierarchy. Most organizations, non and for profit, underscore that power is racialized in favor of white people (Meskil, 2016). Most executives of a company are white and male. And the administrative support most often is Black, Brown, and female. As well, sometimes the learning curve is for those *used to* having their voices heard, used to positions of power, because of their privilege. "At ELNC, people at the top are people of color. And those supporting them are not. It's a flipped script," remarks Powell. Powell explains that if real change in access to quality education is going to work, it has to at least be shared power at all levels. Leadership roles, based on ELNC philosophy, necessarily need to be filled by a significant percentage of people of color.

ELNC has to practice what it preaches in early childhood classrooms as well as in executive leadership circles. Power must be examined and redefined and shared. "How do we look at the power structure," asks Powell, "so that at the minimum it's at least a shared power?" The fact that ELNC centers its mission around such a question of power sharing is very telling, cutting edge. At a macro level, the fact that ELNC seeks to respond to such a question by implementing an inverse model of an organizational chart based on race to upset racial hierarchy as part of its core operations reveals one of the ways in which ELNC sets itself apart. Just as schools communicate to what extent they value inspiring Black and Brown students with Black and Brown teachers (Downer et al., 2016; Hanushek et al., 2005), ELNC communicates to the Grand Rapids community through its staffing just how seriously ELNC aims to do the same among its staff and partners.

The staffing decision to have Ezeh lead ELNC underscores the aim to shift power. Period. Ezeh came to ELNC to build, sustain, and grow the organization based on her academic profile, professional ECE experiential knowledge, and good character. Ezeh formed an organization full of leaders willing to continue learning while doing the ECE work. The W.K. Kellogg Foundation, ELNC partners, and more needed someone from a true village to harness the resources of another village. Ezeh has taken the legacy of her parents – their values and beliefs about their child – and used them to replicate a collaborative model that serves those whom society has written off (Fanon, 1961). In addition, Ezeh has taken what she learned from raising her own children to lead ELNC. Her leadership style defaults to one that comes first from her familial environment, where she expects all children to be educated, cared for, and loved.

References

Bettencourt, A. F., Gross, D., Bower, K., Francis, L., Taylor, K., Singleton, D. L., & Han, H. R. (2020). *Identifying meaningful indicators of parent engagement in early learning for low-income, urban families.* Newbury Park, CA: Sage Journals.

Brown, C. P. (2010). Balancing the readiness equation in early childhood education reform. *Journal of Early Childhood Research*, 8(2), 133–160. https://doi.org/10.1177/1476718X09345504

Ezeh, N. (2020). *Nwaenyi: Child of an elephant: Lessons learned from my father, a Nigerian Chief, about child development and affirmations.* Independently published.

Davoudzadeh, P., McTernan, M. L., & Grimm, K. J. (2015). Early school readiness predictors of grade retention from kindergarten through eighth grade: A multilevel discrete-time survival analysis approach. *Early Child Research Quarterly*, 32, 183–192.

Davy, E. L. (2016). *Culturally responsive leadership: How principals employ culturally responsive leadership to shape the school experiences of marginalized students.* Amsterdam: Amsterdam University Press.

Douglass, A. (2017). *Leading for change in early care and education: Cultivating leadership from within.* New York, NY: Teacher College Press.

Downer, J. T., Goble, P., Myers, S. S., & Pianta, R. C. (2016). Teacher-child racial/ethnic match within pre-kindergarten classrooms and children's early school adjustment. *Early Childhood Research Quarterly*, 37, 26–38. https://doi.org/10.1016/j.ecresq.2016.02.007

Duncan, G. J., Dowsett, C. J., Claessens, A., Magnuson, K., Huston, A. C., Klebanov, P., & Japel, C. (2007). School readiness and later achievement. *Developmental Psychology, 43*, 1428–1445.

Escobar, W. A., Amayah, A. T., & Haque, M. (2021). The role of leaders in catalyzing cooperative behavior in the governance of nonprofit sector shared resources: The case of early childhood education. In D. P. Singh, R. J. Thompson, & K. A. Curran (Eds.), *Reimagining leadership on the commons: Shifting the paradigm for a more ethical, equitable, and just world* (*building leadership bridges*) (pp. 243–253). Emerald Publishing Limited, Bingley.

Fanon, F. (1961). *Les Damnés de la terre*. François Maspero Éditeur.

Garon-Carrier, G., Ansari, A., Letarte, M. J., & Fitzpatrick, C. (2022, August). Early childcare enrollment and the pursuit of higher education: A Canadian longitudinal study. *Learning and Instruction, 80*, 101615.

Grantham-Caston, M., & DiCarlo, C. F. (2021, November 20). Leadership styles in childcare directors. *Early Childhood Education Journal*. https://doi.org/10.1007/s10643-021-01282-2

Halpern, C., Szecsi, T., & Mak, V. (2020, August 18). "Everyone can be a leader": Early childhood education leadership in a center serving culturally and linguistically diverse children and families. *Early Childhood Education Journal, 49*(4), 669–679.

Hanushek, E. A., Kain, J. F., O'Brien, D. M., & Rivkin, S. G. (2005). *The market for teacher quality*. Cambridge, MA: National Bureau of Economic Research. Retrieved from http://www.nber.org/papers/w11154.pdf

Heath, S. B. (1982). What no bedtime story means: Narrative skills at home and school. *Language in Society, 11*(1), 49–76.

Hujala, E. (2019). Leadership in early childhood in times of change: Foreword. In P. Strehmel, J. Heikka, E. Hujala, J. Rodd, & M. Waniganayake (Eds.), *Leadership in early education in times of change: Research from five continents* (pp. 9–13). Toronto, Canada: Barbara Budrich.

Iruka, I. U. (2020). Using a social determinants of early learning framework to eliminate educational disparities and opportunity gaps. In Foundation for Child Development (Ed.), *Getting it right: Using implementation research to improve outcomes in early care and education* (pp. 63–86). New York, NY: Foundation for Child Development.

Jacobson, S., & Notman, R. (2018). Leadership in early childhood education: Implications for parental involvement and student success from New Zealand. *ISEA, 46*(1), 86–100.

Jean-Marie, G., Normore, A., & Mansfield, K. C. (2016). Negotiating race and gender in marginalized work settings. In T. N. Watson & A. H. Normore (Eds.), Racially and ethnically diverse women leading education: A worldview (pp. 35–53). Bingley: Emerald Group Publishing Limited.

Jelks, R. M. (2006). *African Americans in the furniture city: The struggle for civil rights in grand rapids* (illustrated ed.). Champaign: University of Illinois Press.

Jones-Morales, J., & Konrad, A. M. (2018). Attaining elite leadership: Career development and childhood socioeconomic status. *Career Development International, 23*(3), 246–260.

Kagan, S. L., & Hallmark, L. G. (2001). Cultivating leadership in early care and education. *Childcare Information Exchange, 140,* 7–11.

Kay, L. (2022). 'What works' and for whom? Bold Beginnings and the construction of the school ready child. *Journal of Early Childhood Research, 20*(2), 172–184.

Khalifa, M. A. (2018). *Culturally responsive school leadership.* Cambridge, MA: Harvard Education Press.

Ladson-Billings, G. (1995, June). But that's just good teaching! The case for culturally relevant pedagogy. *Theory Into Practice, 34*(3), 159–165.

Lee, R., Han, W. J., Waldfogel, J., & Brooks-Gunn, J. (2018, March 2). Preschool attendance and school readiness for children of immigrant mothers in the United States. *Journal of Early Childhood Research, 16*(2), 190–209. https://doi.org/10.1177/1476718x18761218

Lopez, A. E. (2016, December 9). *Culturally responsive and socially just leadership in diverse contexts: From theory to action* (1st ed.). London: Palgrave Macmillan.

Mariano, M., Santos-Junior, A., Lima, J. L., Perisinotto, J., Brandão, C., Surkan, P. J., & Martins, S. S. (2019, December 26). Ready for school? A systematic review of school readiness and later achievement. *Global Journal of Human-Social Science, 19,* 57–71.

Meskil, D. M. (2016). *A Study of the Perceptions of Racial Equity in One Early Childhood Education Program.* Electronic Theses and Dissertations. Paper 3151. https://dc.etsu.edu/etd/3151

National Association for the Advancement of Colored People. (2022). *Help Black America thrive*. Retrieved October 15, 2022, from https://naacp.org/

National Association for the Education of Young Children. (2020). *Developmentally appropriate practice national association for the education of young children adopted by the NAEYC National Governing Board April 2020*. Retrieved September 25, 2022, from https://www.naeyc.org/sites/default/files/globally-shared/downloads/PDFs/resources/position-statements/dap-statement_0.pdf

Nicholson, J. (2017). *Emphasizing social justice and equity in leadership for early childhood: Taking a postmodern turn to make complexity visible*. Lanham, MD: Lexington Books.

Ramosaj, D. B., & Berisha, M. G. (2014, June 30). Systems theory and systems approach to leadership. *ILIRIA International Review*, 4(1), 59.

Razfar, A., & Gutiérrez, K. (2003). Reconceptualizing early childhood literacy: The sociocultural influence. In J. Larson & J. Marsh (Eds.), *Handbook of early childhood literacy* (pp. 34–47). New York, NY: SAGE Publications.

Ready at Five. (2020). *Readiness matters: 2019–2020 kindergarten readiness assessment report*. Retrieved from https://earlychildhood.marylandpublicschools.org/system/files/filedepot/4/200178_ready5_book_web.pdf

Santamaria, L. J., & Santamaria, A. P. (2016). Toward culturally sustaining leadership: Innovation beyond school improvement promoting equity in diverse contexts. *Education Sciences*, 6(4), Article 33.

Scanlan, M., & López, F. A. (2014, November 6). *Leadership for culturally and linguistically responsive schools* (1st ed.). Abingdon: Routledge.

Shields, C. M. (2010). Transformative leadership: Working for equity in diverse contexts. *Educational Administration Quarterly*, 46(4), 558–589.

Simarasl, N., Tabesh, P., Munyon, T. P., & Marzban, Z. (2022, July). Unveiled confidence: Exploring how institutional support enhances the entrepreneurial self-efficacy and performance of female entrepreneurs in constrained contexts. *European Management Journal*. https://doi.org/10.1016/j.emj.2022.07.003

Smith, N., & Glass, W. (2019). Ready or not? Teachers' perceptions of young children's school readiness. *Journal of Early Childhood Research*, 17(4), 329–346.

Terrell, R. D., Terrell, E. K., Lindsey, R. B., & Lindsey, D. B. (2018, July 6). *Culturally proficient leadership: The personal journey begins within* (2nd ed.). Newbury Park, CA: Corwin.

Watson, T. N., & Normore, A. H. (2016, December 5). *Racially and ethnically diverse women leading education: A world view (Advances in Educational Administration, 25)*. Bingley: Emerald Publishing Limited.

Welsh, J. A., Nix, R. L., Blair, C., Bierman, K. L., & Nelson, K. E. (2010). The development of cognitive skills and gains in academic school readiness for children from low-income families. *Journal of Educational Psychology, 102*(1), 43–53. https://doi.org/10.1037/a0016738

3

Collaboration
Partnering with parents, partnering with place-based organizations

As mentioned in Chapters 1 and 2, ELNC distinguishes itself with a deeply collaborative approach to early childhood education (ECE). Collaboration is not a buzzword for ELNC. It is core to operations where parents and community provide input on programming and work integrally with multiple neighborhood-based organizations. ELNC engages with internal and external stakeholders through a collaborative lens. ELNC debuted by building local partnerships with community members who share the common goal of readying children for kindergarten.

Melita Powell, referenced in Chapter 2, and who is now a program assistant at ELNC, was at the start of ELNC serving as the Program Manager at The Other Way Ministries. In addition, Powell served as ELNC Partners Advisory Committee Co-Chair. "Initially, Dr. Ezeh did work by conducting current reality research around the data to look at early childhood, and find where the gaps were, where the children were who didn't get served," observes Powell. But the very next step, according to Powell, was identifying which organizations could partner with ELNC to reach neighborhood vulnerable children. Ezeh had several main components she was looking for that she knew would be necessary for the community's children to succeed academically.

Trusted

Ezeh selected neighborhood in Grand Rapids that other local organizations and local communities trusted. ELNC success hinged on parental confidence in the ELNC program, which required ELNC to be in regular conversation with neighborhood institutions. Ezeh refers to this sort of relationship as "Institutions of Trust." She aimed to partner with establishments with a proven track record of community-mindedness doing place-based work. By place-based work, Ezeh means drawing from the local and lived community environment and resources with which ELNC's children are familiar. Originally coined by Laurie Lane-Zucker, place-based education can be characterized as a sort of experiential, community-based education. Playgrounds, libraries, gardens, even books, and more are "places" where children can grow their imaginations (Fischer, 2015). In particular, Ezeh was searching for organizations that are commonly called "community-based organizations." Community-based organizations are generalists instead of specialists in one area. They cast a wide net in terms of the services offered but only offer such services to a specific geographic locale (Albarran, 2014). Community-based organizations usually have small operations because they target and are integrated into a single community. Contrary to assumptions, the smallness of community-based organizational geography is a strength and not a weakness (López et al., 2017).

Community-based organizations anchor communities. "They're historical assets," declares Chana Edmond-Verley, former Senior Program Officer for the Doug and Maria DeVos Foundation and current Chief Executive Officer of Vibrant Future. "They are supporting the whole family—that's their secret sauce. They're not in the neighborhood because there's money available. They're there because they're called to be there—and committed to the community." Edmond-Verley's words reinforce that such organizations do not go where the money is, as do many corporations. Community-based organizations go where the community social needs are (Sitienei & Pillay, 2019).

They use money to address decay that leads to weakening of social units such as the family. Community-based organization return on investment is measured by how many families they uplift more so than how enlarged are revenue figures on their balance sheets because they support resource-limited communities (Yakubovich et al., 2016). They are drawn to where there are social breakdowns that they can help build up. They are drawn to areas where institutions are broken but that can also be mended.

There is certain value in a smaller organization that has not always been recognized. "Research is now showing that the smaller organizations are actually having greater outcomes," expresses Edmond-Verley. "Just like a smaller class size, when you can focus in on individuals, you can get to the root [causes of problems and] of [their] solutions." Research (Ho et al., 2016) confirms Verley's observations. Size of a program does matter, having an overt impact on an organization's ability to carry out its mission. In addition, Verley surmises, there is a cultural competence of a neighborhood-rooted organization that speaks to the ways neighborhood people live their lives (Munthali et al., 2014). Community-based organizations, which tend to be smaller organizations, address the needs of the neighborhood using neighborhood methods. These institutions are of value because they are usually staffed with people working right down the block from the people they serve (Adams & McDaniel, 2012). Community-based ECE is localized, relationship-based early childhood education.

Ezeh, as an early childhood expert, led the design of ELNC using relationship-building with children, teachers, parents, and other organizations. For educators, education centers on the quality of relationships between teacher and student. However, in the ELNC model, parents are teachers as much as the paid teaching staff. Relationships with parents are just as, if not more, important than any other relationship at ELNC. Such a premium on relationship with parents supports the success of a community-based model of ECE (Fan et al., 2021). ELNC is an educational organization, which means that ELNC has to reflect an educationist worldview. To provide education services, Ezeh also needed to locate community-based organizations that championed *local* community causes. Ezeh needed to find neighborhood institutions that listened to and learned from the community the way good students listen to and learn from teachers. She knew that building a successful collaborative could only result from the trust of those in need of targeted support services. And trust was exactly what was needed if ELNC wanted parents to trust them with their most valuable assets – their children.

Not the power players

Ezeh also sought to cultivate trust in ELNC by working with those perceived to have little power. One may dub counter-intuitive efforts to partner with the powerless, but Ezeh knew that she needed the endorsement of organizations on the ground actually faithfully doing the work right in the communities that many leaders in high places brag about and take credit for. Ezeh was well aware that ELNC progress was about serving neighbors instead of focusing on getting invited to big tables in high places. ELNC's legacy would be measured ultimately based on the ability to get people who had strong relationships with the families who had small children who could not access quality preschool (Munthali et al., 2014).

Ezeh also knew that stakeholders who were excluded from being "invited to the table" was no indicator of capacity or quality of work on the part of such stakeholders themselves. Having herself spent years being left out of powerful decision-making, despite her stellar academic and professional qualifications, Ezeh was well aware that she needed to search for authentic community organizers whose day-to-day grind speaks to motivation around addressing neighborhood needs rather than simply aiming to pad resumes (Osterling & Garza, 2004). Ezeh needed relationships that empowered children and their parents and not necessarily those who possess impressive profit and loss statements.

Willingness to do things differently

ELNC aimed to be a results-oriented organization. Leadership and other staff have been driven to point to tangible progress regarding giving poor Black and Brown kids access to quality preschool. As a result, ELNC needed to partner with organizations that had a results-oriented organizational history from which ELNC could learn and use to build trust with local communities (Sitienei & Pillay, 2019). Moreover, ELNC desired to build a coalition of sorts with those who were willing to let go of the way things had been done, given that strategies of yesteryears yielded few positive learning results for vulnerable children (Yakubovich et al., 2016). Ezeh needed to liaise with organizations that were willing to be unsettled and to admit to the problems of racial and class segregation that hindered access to education for the community's children (Adams & McDaniel, 2012).

Ezeh needed collaborators that would not only provide early education but would be willing to constantly ask how they could do it differently. She and her associate director K'Sandra Earle sought partners who were open to change and make immediate adjustments. In short, they needed a community team that was humble and honest about what needed to be recalibrated to undercut the 83% abysmal statistic. She needed organizations who refused to let the status quo prevail, continuing to determine the marginalized status of the city's children.

Not territorial

Grand Rapids, Michigan, is a community rich in philanthropy. Accordingly, many nonprofits vie for the same sources of funding to carry out their philanthropic missions (Hall, 2006). Being a true collaborative requires ELNC and other organizations to let go of a scarcity mentality that is based on a sort of Darwinian competition of trying to outdo one another in order to survive (Hall, 2006). ELNC departs from such archaic "struggles for existence" and natural selection because ELNC philosophy is grounded in the notion that all community partners must exist for ELNC to exist. ELNC territory is communal territory. ELNC resources are community resources. ELNC cannot worry about and ultimately obtain sources of funding (Fisher, 2000) without inviting others in to share and use the same funding resources.

The ELNC collaborative is based on the notion that many are stronger than one. It is a sentiment that parallels the Haitian (Kenol, 2010) mantra found on the country's flag: *l'union fait la force* or union makes strength. In other words, ELNC and its community partners believe that there can be no individual ELNC success without working with other organizations. It is the collaborative that gives ELNC and its partners what is needed most. ELNC and its partners need to hold up the needs of the collaborative just as strongly as they hold up the needs of their own respective organizations. There is no "us" versus "them." There is only us *with* them. Those who put the needs of the collaborative side-by-side with the needs of their own organizations realize that they will end up stronger and able to do more for the community. "That's what collaboration is: working together to achieve the same purpose or goal rather than everyone individually fighting to do it on their own," quips Rose Simmons. "Partnering is more collective. It goes further, beyond what we could do on our own. It's harder, but we're stronger when we do it together."

Typically, at the start of any new nonprofit, there are core conversations and standard steps to form the organization (Selden et al., 2006; Sowa, 2009; Tilhou et al., 2018). But with ELNC, there were seven or eight organizations joining in, doing it all together. These seven partners were also already nonprofits on their own, with their own boards, their own missions and goals and visions. "So there had to be some honest conversations," Edmond-Verley asserts. "As one of those organizations, you're growing and engaging with this new thing, but you're also thinking about your own funding base. To truly be at the table as a collaborative, we can't undermine each other." Edmond-Verley argues holding each other accountable, addressing conflicts, and being in communication about those funding sources was important. There had to be open conversations about the ways each organization's funding strategy could impact others in the collaborative – and the collaborative as a whole. So each organization, Edmond-Verley recalls, had to make an intentional decision to not be territorial, to not think only of their own funding needs – and instead think about each other's needs.

Along with a willingness to abandon being territorial about funding, ELNC and her partners needed to abandon being territorial about leadership. While each organization would preserve its original organizational leadership to implement internal goals, the ELNC collaborative structure requires central leadership. This is a shift. A collaborative partner must be willing to follow the leadership of Ezeh when carrying out collaborative objectives. ELNC must function with unity (Tilhou et al., 2020). "They each had to make a conscious decision to approach this new effort without a scarcity mentality," notes Edmond-Verley. The scarcity mentality can be described as a fixed circle with a finite shape or like a pie with only a certain number of pieces to eat. The scarcity mentality assumes there are few resources so each stakeholder must rush and grab the resources whenever they can without regard to whether others need and can access these same resources.

But with a collaborative effort, by working together, Edmond-Verley expresses, "instead the pie can grow." Keeping with this train of thought: "This is the brilliance of ELNC: what happened was by participating in those programs, our capacity as an organization grew," observes Kurt Reppart, former executive director of The Other Way. Reppart reports that because of the collaborative work together, including receiving training to run new programs and develop early education, as well as strengthening organizational skills, The Other Way has grown and is now able to increase their programming outside of its work with ELNC – a capacity that in turn opened them up to greater funding (Fantuzzo et al., 1997).

Such was not the point, Reppart reveals. But that is what happened as collaborative leaders were willing to put aside any territorial concerns and be open to how they could grow as partners – how they could work together to better serve the families in their neighborhood.

> They pick the right partners: place-based partners that are embedded in communities and know the neighborhood.

That's a big part of it—that we know the neighborhood and ELNC trusts that. And we trust *them* that they're the experts in early childhood, declares Reppart.

We really had to depend on each other. ELNC wouldn't be able to get to the finish line without us. And we would never be able to get all the accreditations without ELNC. So it's this fantastic mutual respect. We wade through the hard things together and we don't walk away from the table. That's why it works.

Reppart's comments reinforce the *l'union fait la force* leadership perspective. ELNC had to depend on others with historical knowledge of the community (Walzer et al., 2016). And others had to depend on ELNC who possessed the academic chops for partners to gain a level of recognition by institutions who can increase the likelihood that partnerships are sustained long-term (Adams & McDaniel, 2012; Adger, 2001).

Besides collaboration with other institutions, as mentioned previously, ELNC needed to collaborate with parents. Proceeding to design early childhood programs could only take place once a group of organizations were all in agreement about community goals and after having the consent of parents of children (López et al., 2017). The next step was collaboration with the parents and community whose children would be in ELNC classrooms.

While this step might seem obvious, ELNC was charting new territory with formal integration of parents into early childhood programs (Graue et al., 2004). Parents were the people who knew their children's needs better than anyone else, after all. Ezeh was intent on re-establishing the parents as the leaders in their own children's education. To truly do that, ELNC needed to make sure learning from parents was an important step *before* making program design decisions. Parents' input would need to be an integral resource for those decisions. ELNC engaged the community by simple but very intentionally designed *listening* (Compton-Lilly & Delbridge, 2018), per Sharon Killebrew. "Just listening." Killebrew explains that this stemmed from the understanding that parents are a child's first teacher. "Dr. Ezeh pulled together community forums with parents at each level," she says.

> That's what was really unique about it: what do the parents think? What do the grassroots organizations think? What does the community think? What did the teachers think? What will it look like if we get it right? That was the key: asking the questions and then listening to the answers.

These and other questions about parental involvement (Osterling & Garza, 2004) into the formal structure of early childhood programming needed to be asked in order to move into program design.

ELNC got answers to questions about what children needed to maximize learning potential in the classrooms from parents and neighbors. In addition, ELNC became aware of obstacles that – beyond number of available classrooms – were making it harder for children to attend preschool. Transportation, language barrier, and having an instructor of record whom one can trust in the classroom all rose to the top of what needs to be met for regular attendance (Fan et al., 2021).

ELNC work with parents revealed historical hurdles to accessing preschool and helped the team discover strengths in the community and its families. "I can't build on deficits," maintains Chana Edmond-Verley about the importance of this approach.

> I can build on strengths. No one scaffolds up a wall when the wall is crumbling. They figure out where the strength is in the wall and they scaffold from there. Accessing all forms of knowledge and capacity are what—when you have a level of unbiased and competence—you can design from strengths.

Edmond-Verley's sentiments reveal that no matter how bad things may appear to be, one must always look for that which is good. These children coming from homes with few financial resources or education means that they bring other possibilities to the educational space (Iruka et al., 2022). They come from families that care deeply about their children's education. These children are willing to learn but perhaps just need to learn in ways that are conducive to who they are as learners more so that who their teachers are as teachers (Lamb, 2020).

A culturalist approach is a huge part of providing learning opportunities that are commensurate with how learners learn (Ladson-Billings, 2006). Working with parents to unearth program design needs and strengths also, importantly, gave ELNC a wealth of opportunities to further understand and honor cultural norms of learner home life. Instead of judging information about cultures as right or wrong, they were unearthing information to springboard from. "Better understanding of communities gave insight into what the culture honored and respected," affirms Edmond-Verley. "And then they designed ways to honor that cultural perspective. How powerful is that?" The power in culture is real. As explained earlier, defaulting to culture as the analytic framework for supporting learners at ELNC stems from Ezeh's Nigerian and immigrant background. She only views learners through the lens she views herself.

As addressed earlier, Ezeh's village upbringing in Nigeria paved the way for her to use culture as her approach to understanding each child at ELNC. Culturally, in Nigeria, the ways of a child points back to the ways of a child's parents. The variability in parents' cultural identities accounts for one way of understanding variability in the academic performance of children (Ogbu, 1987). In short, understand parents to understand the child. Clearly, the result of a culturalist approach, particularly within an early childhood frame, lends to parental involvement (Banks & Banks, 1993; Nieto, 2017). This work with parents, which went against the grain of much early childhood programs, was essential to ELNC's success. Honor the parents to honor the child. "Parents are an untapped resource that we haven't fully capitalized on. They have agency and they care even more than we do about their children. So they are a resource to be leveraged," comments Edmond-Verley. "There's nothing more powerful than all the adults being on the same page for a child, all focused on what the child needs to be successful." From an ELNC perspective, being on the same page means all stakeholders knowing the culture of each child in part by getting to know parents and designing learning experience around such cultural knowledge.

According to ELNC constituents, how one engages parents makes all the difference. "Even the way that you brought the parents together had to be very intentional to show that you valued what they had to say," explains Killebrew.

> So you brought them together in a nice place, you showed them that their opinion mattered, then asked the questions very open-ended. You asked questions like 'What's the hardest thing about raising your child?' and 'What's the hardest thing about getting them to preschool?' and 'What do you value?'

Once again, a cornerstone of ELNC development is asking questions and asking the right ones as they pertain to parents. These questions reveal that ELNC parental involvement is predicated on knowing what hurdles parents face to educate their children at home and beyond. System-level changes demand everyone involved – especially having the parents be on the same page regarding what early learning should look like for their child. ELNC focused on parents as the first teacher (Albarran, 2014), knowing that parents already had within them the best learning solutions to the problem of vulnerable children entering kindergarten not "ready to learn."

Learning solutions had to be cross-sector (Tilhou et al., 2020). The sum of collective energy had to be beyond the purview of any one agency, organization, or discipline. ELNC arose as a collaborative of seven unique grassroots organizations, serving diverse populations, and working in collaboration with parents. ELNC was a communal development opportunity, which helped to create and unify commitments to significant, sustainable improvements in ECE and equity (Nicholson, 2017; Santamaria & Santamaria, 2016) outcomes.

The collaborative structure of ELNC promotes an environment of diverse thinking and problem solving among stakeholders composed of parents, partners, ELNC leadership, its board, social justice-geared philanthropists, and more. Where many systems (Bruns et al., 2017; Ramosaj & Berisha, 2014) in organizations develop strategies based on theory and supposition, ELNC does so based on the practical experience and knowledge gained from its partners over decades of relationship-building with vulnerable families living in their neighborhoods.

Based on research (Kaplan & Larkin, 2003; Pears & Kim, 2021), ELNC took a "two-generational" approach to preparing children for success. The organization was working to not only prepare the community's children for success but its parents as well (Albarran, 2014). In sum, ELNC is not just designed for child success but is in fact designed for overall family success. As a child's first teacher, a parent must be supported to be viewed as empowered to lead the education of their own child (Connor et al., 2005).

Traditionally, education has focused most on the child (Xu, 2018). ELNC's methodology, focusing on parents and restoring the parents' role in their child's education, was a huge shift in understanding of what educational success would look like (Figures 3.1 and 3.2). This method came to be known as the EPIC model: "Empowering Parents, Impacting Children."

The strategies employed in EPIC model were intentionally designed to be a parent-driven, two-generational approach employing existing community collaborative resources. The model is founded on the understanding that it is critical that early learning be viewed from both bottom-up and top-down lenses, ensuring that targeted neighborhoods can have a strong voice and actively participate in shaping their children's future.

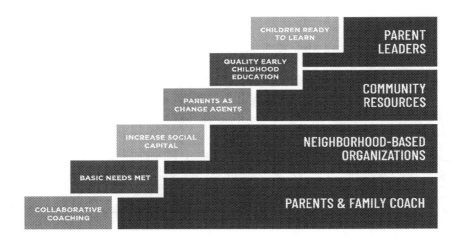

EMPOWERING PARENTS IMPACTING CHILDREN (EPIC)

Intentionally designed strategies for a "Parent Driven," two-generational approach utilizing existing community collaborative resources.

MODEL DEVELOPED BY PONA CONSULTING, L3C

FIGURE 3.1 ELNC embraces a dual-generational approach embedding the EPIC Model within the framework of all ELNC Early Childhood Education programs. The core strategy of the EPIC model is to provide support, through the services of a Family Coach, to families as they identify and address barriers preventing them from meeting their basic needs and developing social capital, relying heavily on existing community resources. EPIC is the promoter of higher levels of community among staff, and accountability among parents (regarding attendance and community with site staff).

EPIC MODEL PROCESS

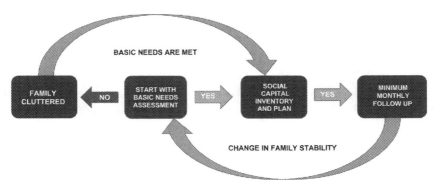

MODEL DEVELOPED BY PONA CONSULTING, L3C

FIGURE 3.2 EPIC Model Process "Arrows."

References

Adams, G., & McDaniel, M. (2012). *Untapped potential: Partnering with community-based organizations to support participation of lower-incidence immigrant communities in the Illinois preschool for all initiative.* Washington, DC: Urban Institute.

Adger, C. T. (2001). School-community-based organization partnerships for language minority students' school success. *Journal of Education for Students Placed at Risk, 6*(1–2), 7–25.

Albarran, A. S. (2014). *Improving school readiness through parent education programming: Understanding the role of community-based organizations in a large urban city center.* ProQuest LLC, Ann Arbor, MI.

Banks, J. A., & Banks, C. A. M. (Eds.). (1993). *Multicultural education: Issues and perspectives.* Boston, MA: Allyn and Bacon.

Bruns, D. A., LaRocco, D. J., Sharp, O. L., & Sopko, K. M. (2017). Leadership competencies in U.S. early intervention/early childhood special education service systems: A national survey. *Infants & Young Children, 30*(4), 304–319.

Compton-Lilly, C., & Delbridge, A. (2018). What can parents tell us about poverty and literacy learning? Listening to parents over time. *Journal of Adolescent & Adult Literacy, 62*(5), 531–539.

Connor, C. M., Son, S.-H., Hindman, A. H., & Morrison, F. J. (2005). Teacher qualifications, classroom practices, family characteristics, and preschool experience: Complex effects on first graders' vocabulary and early reading outcomes. *Journal of School Psychology, 43,* 343–375.

Fan, X., Linder, S., D'Amico, L. K., White, K. M., & Pawloski, T. (2021, May 18). Identifying the needs of prekindergarten children: A focus on health, wellbeing, and family environment. *Early Childhood Education Journal, 50*(5), 823–840. https://doi.org/10.1007/s10643-021-01206-0

Fantuzzo, J., Childs, S., Hampton, V., Ginsburg-Block, M., Coolahan, K. C., & Debnam, D. (1997). Enhancing the quality of early childhood education: A follow-up evaluation of an experiential, collaborative training model for head start. *Early Childhood Research Quarterly, 12*(4), 425–437. https://doi.org/10.1016/s0885-2006(97)90020-x

Fischer, S. (2015). Playing in literary landscapes: Considering children's need for fantasy literature in the place-based classroom. *Occasional Paper Series*, *2015*(33).

Fisher, H. (2000). *Federal funding for early childhood supports and services: A guide to sources and strategies*. Chicago, IL: ERIC.

Graue, E., Clements, M. A., Reynolds, A. J., & Niles, M. D. (2004). More than teacher directed or child initiated: Preschool curriculum type, parent involvement, and children's outcomes in the Child-Parent Centers. *Education Policy Analysis Archives*, *12*(72), 1–40.

Hall, P. D. (2006). A historical overview of philanthropy, voluntary associations, and nonprofit organizations in the United States, 1600–2000. *The nonprofit sector: A research handbook*, *2*, 32–65.

Ho, D., Lee, M., & Teng, Y. (2016). Size matters: The link between staff size and perceived organizational support in early childhood education. *International Journal of Educational Management*, *30*(6), 1104–1122.

Iruka, I. U., Cabrera, N., & Páez, M. (2022). Supporting and engaging with diverse families during the early years: Emerging approaches that matter for children and families. *Early Childhood Research Quarterly*, *60*, 390–393. https://doi.org/10.1016/j.ecresq.2022.04.001

Kaplan, M., & Larkin, E. (2003). Launching intergenerational programs in early childhood settings: A comparison of explicit intervention with an emergent approach. *Early Childhood Education Journal*, *31*(3), 157–163. https://doi.org/10.1023/b:ecej.0000012133.71718.2b

Kenol, B. (2010). Haiti: Sustaining hope in suffering hearts. *Spiritan Magazine*, *34*(1), 5.

Ladson-Billings, G. (2006). Yes, but how do we do it? Practicing culturally relevant pedagogy. In J. Landsman & C. W. Lewis (Eds.), *White teachers/diverse classrooms: A guide to building inclusive schools, promoting high expectations, and eliminating racism* (pp. 29–42). Sterling, VA: Stylus.

Lamb, I. (2020, August 2). Are early childhood educators in Southern Ontario being sufficiently prepared for teaching Indigenous students? *Journal of Early Childhood Research*, *19*(1), 55–69. https://doi.org/10.1177/1476718x20942940

López, M., Hofer, K., Bumgarner, E., & Taylor, D. (2017). *Developing culturally responsive approaches to serving diverse populations: A resource guide for community-based organizations*. National Research Center on Hispanic Children and Families, Publication No. 2017-17.

Munthali, A. C., Mvula, P. M., & Silo, L. (2014). Early childhood development: The role of community based childcare centres in Malawi. *SpringerPlus, 3*(1), 1–10.

Nicholson, J. (2017). *Emphasizing social justice and equity in leadership for early childhood: Taking a postmodern turn to make complexity visible*. Lanham, MD: Lexington Books.

Nieto, S. (2017). Re-imagining multicultural education: New visions, new possibilities*. *Multicultural Education Review, 9*, 1–10.

Ogbu, J. U. (1987). Variability in minority school performance: A problem in search of explanation. *Anthropology and Education Quarterly, 18*, 312–334.

Osterling, J. P., & Garza, A. (2004). Strengthening Latino parental involvement forming community-based organizations/school partnership. *NABE Journal of Research and Practice, 2*(1), 270–284.

Pears, K. C., & Kim, H. (2021). *A two-generational approach to promoting a successful transition to kindergarten* (pp. 322–340). Hindawi.

Ramosaj, D. B., & Berisha, M. G. (2014, June 30). Systems theory and systems approach to leadership. *ILIRIA International Review, 4*(1), 59.

Santamaria, L. J., & Santamaria, A. P. (2016). Toward culturally sustaining leadership: Innovation beyond school improvement promoting equity in diverse contexts. *Education Sciences, 6*(4), Article 33.

Selden, S., Sowa, J., & Sandfort, J. (2006). The impact of nonprofit collaboration in early child care and education on management and program outcomes. *Public Administration Review, 66*(3), 412–425.

Sitienei, E. C., & Pillay, J. (2019). Psychosocial support for orphans and vulnerable children in a community-based organization in Kericho, Kenya. *Journal of Children's Services, 14*(4), 292–302.

Sowa, J. (2009). The collaboration decision in nonprofit organizations: Views from the front line. *Nonprofit and Voluntary Sector Quarterly, 38*(6), 1003–1025.

Tilhou, R., Rose, B., Eckhoff, A., & Glasgow, J. (2018). Building partnerships: The role of nonprofit organizations in supporting education diplomacy in early childhood. *Childhood Education, 94*(3), 84–89.

Tilhou, R., Eckhoff, A., & Rose, B. (2020, March 21). A collective impact organization for early childhood: Increasing access to quality care by uniting community sectors. *Early Childhood Education Journal*, *49*(1), 111–123.

Walzer, N., Weaver, L., & McGuire, C. (2016). Collective impact approaches and community development issues. *Community Development*, *47*(2), 156–166.

Xu, Y. (2018, December 5). Engaging families of young children with disabilities through family-school-community partnerships. *Early Child Development and Care*, *190*(12), 1959–1968. https://doi.org/10.1080/03004430.2018.1552950

Yakubovich, A. R., Sherr, L., Cluver, L. D., Skeen, S., Hensels, I. S., Macedo, A., & Tomlinson, M. (2016). Community-based organizations for vulnerable children in South Africa: Reach, psychosocial correlates, and potential mechanisms. *Children and Youth Services Review*, *62*, 58–64.

4

Values

As touched on briefly in previous chapters, the Early Learning Neighborhood Collaborative (ELNC) approach to early childhood education (ECE) stems from certain organizational values. ELNC's staffing, structure, and foundation speaks to specific values. Organizational values determine the organizational roadmap and vice versa (Salminen, 2017). Values guide choices. Values direct what organizations keep and discard to maintain operations.

Core ELNC values include outcomes, cultural competence, creativity and innovation, place-based classroom settings, and two-generational programming. Of course, each one of these values do not function independently. No one value can be selected on its own for application in an ELNC setting. These values overlap. These values are mutually inclusive. They work in sync to implement the ELNC mission and vision. Notwithstanding, understanding ELNC requires understanding each value as a unique unit that contributes to the larger collaborative structure.

Outcomes

It's essential to measure organizational and classroom progress as well as individual children's progress.

Measurable evidence of children's increasing knowledge, skills, and abilities indicates level of program success. Such evidence holds classrooms, teachers, parents, and the entire organization accountable. Outcomes reveal what learners at ELNC know and what they don't. Values direct to where ELNC will focus its resources. What is working for children and what is not becomes apparent based on the extent to which ELNC learners have reached learning outcomes. "We live in a culture (the United States), that deals with data every day," observes Ezeh. She notes that many in the community were aware of the data behind educational success rates and preparedness rates, but it was too easy to highlight the data without any action in response. "That's a sign of injustice: you know something is wrong, but you're not doing anything about it." The extent to which learners at ELNC demonstrate knowledge of learning outcomes is part of the extent to which ELNC can claim to be engaging in justice-oriented ECE.

Ezeh underscores that data is part of everyday operations in the education sphere. Without the data, ELNC cannot know to what extent their programming accurately reflects their ELNC outcomes value. Accordingly, collection and analysis of data needed to be present. There were two sets of data that jump-started ELNC's formation. The first was the Grand Rapids Public Schools (GRPS)'s release of the 83% statistic: a full 83% of children going into kindergarten in GRPS were not ready for school. The second came out of further investigation after hearing this first figure. Data collected about learner achievement in Grand Rapids Public Schools, discussed in Chapters 1 and 2, revealed that only two out of ten children had access to ECE. "When we started, our goal was to close that gap," remarks Ezeh.

> So of course, we want to make sure that our outcomes, informed by data, are then informing our practice. We wanted to measure for questions like: how are the children doing? How many slots have we created? How do we know that they're ready for kindergarten at the end of their time in our program? ELNC is fighting to make sure we reverse that trend.

The value of measuring organizational and individual learner progress mandates collecting data regularly. Achieving outcomes at ELNC, like other work at the organization, stems from the questions raised. Ezeh and her program team, anchored by K'Sandra Earle, recognize the need for socio-emotional, academic, enrollment, family engagement and support, and other outcomes as a basis for ELNC legitimacy in early childhood services.

Multi-faceted, measurable outcomes must be a value of ELNC to curtail historical inequities. The success of reaching the goal to lower the 83% figure highlighted and raise the two out of ten rate of students ready for primary school can only be measured if ELNC values outcomes. Tracking progress must be in place, as must investment in the cost of mining the data. Tracking data entails more than measuring success at the end. It is also about paying close attention throughout the learning process to know how to adjust, improve, and continue to adjust. In other words, diagnostic and formative data are on par with summative data (Lungu et al., 2021). Only by surveying diverse data sources to identify if outcomes have been met can the organization grow.

The ELNC has three major checkpoints to track individual student progress. All data tracking individual progress is added into a database to track entire cohorts of learners for the academic year. The purpose is to review the information for learning trends including but not limited to gaps in learning. At the beginning of the year, there is a pre-assessment to measure baseline skills and aptitudes before children start their education at ELNC. In the spring, a midway assessment is administered to measure the same skills and aptitudes measured in the fall. The second assessment captures positive and negative achievement growth. Logically, post-assessments round out the assessment schedule at the end of the academic year. This sort of comprehensive data gathering offers a panoramic view of cohort learner progress and lack thereof. Consistent with other educational institutions, ELNC can confidently throughout the academic year identify success of program offerings for children based on sound evidence collected. Data collections and analysis drive program improvement. Data collected can be employed to help enrolled students who are struggling as well as those slated to be part of the incoming program cohort the following year.

Moreover, ELNC tracks data of families. ELNC conducts Basic Needs Assessment (BNA) of all our families to help understand how the child is ultimately doing based on homelife. How the family is doing is the central question to be answered by the BNA. Based on the BNA, ELNC creates a family centered plan to work on together to address family needs. Data, zeroing in closely on measured outcomes, not only provides donors and other support stakeholders with pertinent information about operational progress but also with tangible facts about how ELNC can constantly grow. ELNC's sole purpose is educational success for all children and their families. And data tracking renders renders ELNC accountable in its efforts to achieve such an equity-oriented goal.

This attention to outcomes (Infurna, 2020) and consistently measuring the learning success and challenges of ELNC programs has resulted in ELNC preschool classrooms getting the highest ratings from the state of Michigan, with a stunning success rate of 91% readiness for kindergarten for ELNC preschool graduates.

Creativity and innovation

ELNC works to find and use new and different objectives, strategies, and activities to help their children thrive.

Initial programming did not drive this value. Creativity and innovation are values for any stakeholder interested in better achievement results at any stage of organizational planning. Accordingly, ELNC does not package and market creativity and innovation for new ECE programs. ELNC staff default to creativity and innovation as part of day-to-day operations. As a child and parent-centered organization, ELNC functions with regular input from each cohort of families each academic year. In fact, failure to recognize that needs and environments change can stunt organizational development (van Oers, 2013).

Valuing creativity and innovation also speaks to humility in one's educational approach. Good educators are always learning. Educators are life-long learners. "Therefore, lifelong learning involves a continuous learning process, acquiring and expanding skills, behaviours and knowledge throughout the life of an individual" (Mawas & Muntean, 2018, p. 1). One cannot assume to know all that is necessary for schooling, that the answers are available, that the right solution can be discovered. Humility centers on a willingness to keep learning and growing, to seek new solutions and improve, and to listen (King, 2010).

Valuing creativity and innovation allowed ELNC to address key elements of successful programming:

Bigger is not better. Partners at ELNC recognized early on that having one big ECE location would not serve the needs of diverse families (Cleveland et al., 2006; Jose et al., 2021). Transportation is one of the main factors determining access to preschool for children, particularly if families are not within walking distance of an early childhood center location (Sattin-Bajaj, 2022). Families possess varying types of transportation to no transportation at all (McCarthy et al., 2017) that impact if and how children can attend school (Kocyigit, 2015). Few families would likely be able to participate in ELNC programs if one central ELNC location existed (Halgunseth, 2009). No matter how elaborate of a building, the families ELNC claims to serve would be underserved without ELNC also providing means to access the location of ELNC services (Lenhoff et al., 2022). "It could be the most beautiful place on earth, but if our kids don't have access to it, then it's not going to help them," opines Ezeh. Accordingly, "ELNC intentionally partnered with community-based organizations to add little schools or 'La Escuelita' throughout the neighborhoods." "Doing so not only increased accessibility for families but actually became easier to monitor and manage progress and provided place-based experience for our children" Ezeh reflects. Decentralized access has proved to be essential for families participating in ELNC programs.

Collaboration. Partner organizations maintain their independent institutional identities while working cross-institutionally.

Deep collaboration allows for exploration of new ways to serve learners and their families with operational conditions that speak to a variety of perspectives and knowledge bases.

Parent teachers. Educational research (Jeon et al., 2018; McLaughlin, 2020; Pasini, 2018; Powell, 1998; Raynal et al., 2021; Varshney et al., 2020) overwhelmingly supports direct parental involvement in their children's educational achievement. Ezeh, as an experienced educator and intellectual, was aware of how much parents must be consulted and be an integral part of implementing ELNC's curriculum. In addition, parents were necessary to develop and sustain the value of cultural competence, particularly with a roadblock of finding teachers who *looked like* the children they were teaching (Rasheed et al., 2019). ELNC championed parent teachers, where K'Sandra and her program team selected certain parents of children in the program, train them to assist the lead teacher as a paraprofessional, providing leadership from a person of color and the cultural competence to help the lead teacher make sure they were meeting the cultural value of students. "Children need someone to look up to and relate to," affirms Ezeh. "And I will tell you: the stress level of the parents went down when a parent teacher was in the room. Their shoulders visibly relaxed." Knowing that there are biological (or foster) parents of other students in the classroom reassures parents that their children are not only learning what they need to but are being well cared for in the process. In this sense, parents have the confidence that, because parents play an important role in the program, the community as a whole is educating their children.

Family coaches

In addition to parent teachers, ELNC uses family coaches. The education of the child is a matter of the education of the family. "A child does not exist alone. A child exists within the context of a family," acknowledges Ezeh. "For you to properly educate a child, you need to pay attention to the family—and that's where the family coaches come in." Family coaches are graduates of social work or family studies who work with parents on connecting to resources for basic needs and building social capital. They have supported parents who in turn were able to put even more focus on supporting their own children (Jayaraman et al., 2015). One of the predictors of educational achievement is the education of a child's parents. The quality of a child's teachers, the socio-economic status of their family, and the education of parents are usually the biggest determinants of how well a child does in school (Alexandersen et al., 2021). Researchers Debra M. Pacchiano, Maureen R. Wagner, and Holly Lewandowski with Stacy B. Ehrlich and Amanda G. Stein (2018) of the University of Chicago Consortium on School Research write "Simply put, strongly organized programs created contexts far more supportive of teaching, learning and family engagement than the contexts created by weakly organized programs" (p. 1). Based on research, family coaches are a basic, logical step for positive learner achievement.

Even with family coaches available to all families, ELNC remains humble to the fact that each family needs targeted assistance. "Anybody who's heard me speak about ELNC has heard me say 'We are building the plane as we fly it,'" explains Ezeh. "That gives us permission to be innovative. We don't have a one size fits all for all families that we're working with. If it [a service] does not work for this family, with her input, we change it around." In other words, family coaches must be employed in ways that are commensurate with the needs of parents and their children. However, ELNC learned about the need for family coaches, and targeted use of them, much later in ELNC's development. Family coaches were not part of original program design, but with their continued deployment increases the optimal services ELNC provides learners (Hnasko, 2020). Moreover, family coaches add flexibility and growth (Page & Eadie, 2019). One preschool, for example, had parents asking for half-day preschool when preschool was first offered. But then, just a few years later, the parents all had full-time jobs and were requesting full-time preschool. With the assistance of family coaches, ELNC adjusted preschool to be a full-time schooling experience.

90 ◆ Values

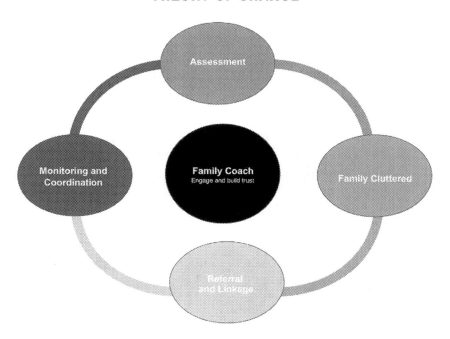

MODEL DEVELOPED BY PONA CONSULTING, L3C

FIGURE 4.1 Family Coach.

Parent teachers and family coaches in the *little schools/La Escuelitas* have become a winning formula. The Little Schools/LaEscuelitas are supported by the work of families in the neighborhoods. "And that's why having little schools Little Schools/LaEscuelitas in the neighborhood is very important: because you're able to make those changes," explains Ezeh. ELNC's small-school innovation approach with parent teachers and family coaches is different than a traditional institutional education approach in large part because parents have much more power in their children's education than what is normative in schools (Einarsdottir & Jónsdóttir, 2019). Parents not only enrich ELNC program service offerings; they are part of program services that support ELNC's creative and innovative model of early learning.

Families are not an add-on to the little school or *Escuelita*. They are the little school or *Escuelita*, along with the children themselves. Thus, parents are an essential part of the ELNC model. Teachers, administrators, and other staff work with the advice, counsel, and leadership of families in neighborhood communities to constantly recalibrate, innovate, and celebrate the learning of kids (Barnett, 2010; Bigras, 2010; Cleveland et al., 2006; Manz, 2012; Figure 4.1).

Cultural competence

Children grow and develop best when learning is consistent with the cultural rhythms and patterns of their families, of their communities.

A one-size-fits-all approach to education may be easier for educators, but ELNC knows that doing so does not honor the complexity of families and learning (Cumming et al., 2015). The popular education mantra that all children can learn (Leverett, 2006) is best understood that all kids can really learn but in ways that may not be familiar to or comfortable for educators. And culture becomes one of the unfamiliar ways in which educators must support learning.

A leading approach to cultural competency is to have teachers, in fact, to have most of all leaders in the classroom and school, be people who look like the children they teach. There is far too much scholarship, research, and experience in the field of education that supports having teachers and school staff actually look like and know about the cultural norms of learners in the same classrooms to overlook the importance of cultural competency (Rasheed et al., 2019). "It's not just about the kids learning in their communities. It's also important for children to be taught by people who look like them," explains Pastor Earle. "Cultural competency is an ongoing challenge because the pool of qualified teachers is very limited when it comes to the diversity that should be there." The unfortunate reality is teacher education programs throughout the state of Michigan and the United States are dominated by enrollees who are usually white, female, English only-speaking (Lee, 2013). Approximately 90% of all pre-K-12 teachers are white women

(Allen-Handy & Farinde-Wu, 2017), and the number of white women educators is most pronounced in ECE.

Nadia Brigham, explains the psychology and benefit behind valuing cultural competency, and in particular the value and unique skill set that teachers of color bring to their classrooms. "Teachers of color bring a healthy racial identity formation for children," maintains Brigham. The benefit of having a teacher of color is not just for students of color. White children, she explains, also benefit from having teachers of color. "It helps them to see people of color in leadership roles, and to build relationships with people of color outside the narratives and norms that they will encounter in their life." In essence, providing teachers of color for *all* children, staff, and stakeholders is a direct and measurable way to shift the racist assumptions in a community. All education stakeholders benefit from cultural competency that is also by default, anti-racist (Iruka et al., 2022).

Cultural competency in the classroom includes, importantly, making the extra effort to have teachers of color. Racial and ethnic matching has benefits (Rasheed et al., 2019), as explained above. However, this is just one step to be a culturally competent classroom. Another step is to create a classroom that fits with and honors the culture of its students.

Consider the example of Latinx cultural structures where tight family bonds are paramount (Vesely et al., 2014). Children stay with family when they are young. They stay close to people that the parents know that they can trust, including extended family members (Moreno & Gaytán, 2013). A preschool classroom within a Latino neighborhood will only be successful if it recognizes the value of the Latin familial culture and incorporates such familial approaches into the curriculum (Cycyk & Hammer, 2020). For instance, the practice of adding parent teachers into the classroom came out of listening to and learning from those in the Latino culture. "We put a parent teacher in the classroom," explains Sharon Killebrew, as a means to show the neighborhood that neighborhood culture drives ELNC curriculum and instruction (Horm et al., 2017). Parents have the confidence that what their children are learning at school affirms what children are experiencing at home. "Parents, then, can see that their own cultural values are being respected," observes Killebrew.

Despite much scholarship on cultural competency (Lino, 2016; Porterfield & Scott-Little, 2019; Sinclair, 2021; West-Olatunji et al., 2008) and the simple act of respecting and understanding the culture of children and their families, there is a paucity of using culture to learn in many early childhood classrooms. Ask any Latino or Black person with a Spanish or African name what their experience has been in their early years of schooling and beyond (Keller & Franzak, 2016). Many will say they have a story of their name being grossly mispronounced or altogether changed to be "Americanized" even by teachers to accommodate the culture of the teacher over and above the culture of the learner (Lee, 2013).

This disregard for a learner's own name shows a disregard and disrespect for the same learner's culture. Lack of respect for a child's culture is lack of respect for the child (Moore et al., 2020). Educators who want children to be successful in school know that children must possess self-respect, self-worth. Cultural competency of teachers and staff in the classroom builds respect for the whole child (Arthur et al., 2017).

Cultural competency also recognizes that not everyone has the same structural worldview, meaning-making, and familiarity with stories and other content (Worthington & van Oers, 2017). Every culture has their own language, their own stories, and their own shared knowledge base. Walking into a classroom expecting children from another culture to be familiar and comfortable with the culture of the teacher can lead to cultural and other disconnects between student and teacher (Arndt, 2018). This cultural disconnect may impede learning progression (Sullivan, 2016). The child has to take extra time to learn cultural cues of the teacher in order to carry out tasks of, for instance, learning even new high-frequency words, counting, and reading stories.

> I can't expect children, who are for the most part Spanish-speaking, to be able to know Little Red Riding Hood (1983) or Itsy Bitsy Spider (1998), just because most white children do. You have to realize the background and take that into account,

observes Deisy Madrigal, former Program Director at the Hispanic Center of West Michigan. Some children might instead be more familiar with Anansi the Spider (1987) or Martina the Beautiful Cockroach (2014). Folktales and other genres of stories that have been passed down for generations in communities of learners in a classroom should be part of curricular offerings as a form of cultural competency.

There are a number of considerations when one is designing curriculum and implementing it for Latinx populations. Learners of Latinx heritage are usually vacillating in and out of two distinct cultures and languages.

> Latino children are learning two cultures and two languages. Their little brains are like sponges, but sometimes this dual learning will mean they will score lower in the beginning. But we know that later, they will score higher. It's important that we as educators nurture their first language, and teach them that they should have pride in their culture. We shouldn't just push their culture and language aside, declares Madrigal.

The research on language and content learning supports the quote above (Echevarria et al., 2017). Granted, not every educator speaks Spanish, nor should he or she be required to – a position that the field of education has debated (Garrity et al., 2021; Shannon, 2010). But those who do have knowledge of *el idioma castellano* should employ it in classrooms where it is the home language of enrolled Latinx learners. Quality ECE centers on leading teaching with the language and culture of the learners in front of the teachers (Bergroth & Palviainen, 2016).

Place-based

The best environment for early child education is a child's own neighborhood, town, or community.

In addition to cultural competency, ECE curriculum should honor children's immediate environment. Honoring children is in part a matter of honoring where they actually stay and play. As discussed in Chapter 3, central to ELNC's success is a place-based approach. Each classroom functions based in part on using the local community as a learning resource. "Stick your 3-year-old on a bus and send them out of their community? We've got everything we need *here* to help them," argues Boals. Transportation, as previously mentioned, has been a real barrier to access to quality ECE. As at other levels of education, busing programs emerged as a de facto strategy for early learners living near weak or non-existent preschool programs to participate in school with the hope that such transportation logistics would positively impact learning and development. Traveling across town was the norm when there was reliable transportation. Few leaders actively sought to develop neighborhood institutions. Even centralized locations as a perceived equitable solution could not, as has been discussed, be an equitable option. Many families just do not have the resources to travel beyond their own communities for learning and other opportunities (Cloney et al., 2016). ELNC seeks to support families in their own neighborhoods.

ELNC values the importance of a child's school being in their own neighborhood. Along with removing a significant amount of the transportation barrier, keeping a school in a neighborhood speaks volumes about the value of a neighborhood school for the neighborhood itself. "Neighborhoods can own their children's success," Boals discusses. "We have everything we need here for success for our children." The belief that everything needed for children's success is right in their own neighborhood is important not only for a positive attitude toward children as a learner but also for a positive attitude toward a child as a member of his or her own community. "Your place is good enough" translates to "you are good enough." This very value of "place" is key to learner success (Cloney et al., 2016). Local neighborhoods have what they need to provide quality learning for children. Given that children are born ready to learn, access is usually the missing ingredient to ensure children get the opportunity to learn. Developing preschool institutions to serve local Black and Brown neighborhoods is about honoring and valuing "place" and "space" of Black and Brown kids.

Collaborative partners must also value place-based education. The Other Way's former executive director Kurt Reppart explains that this shift to "you are capable of success right where you are, who you are" is one that is not always at the core of the ways nonprofit organizations approach the people they serve. ELNC has been determined to change such a perspective. "We want to be about empowerment," proclaims Reppart, "rather than charity or mercy." Empowerment says you are capable. Charity says you need a handout to survive. One approach is about agency. The other approach is about dependency. One approach is spoon-feeding. The other is giving the spoon so members can feed themselves. ELNC possesses confidence that children's families can feed themselves as long as they have the spoons to do so.

New Hope Baptist Church also possesses an organizational structure and values that seek to find spoons so that communities can feed themselves. "We've been intentional about providing this resource right where the children live. We want families to know they don't have to leave their community to find quality: they can have quality right where they live," notes Pastor Earle. Put another way, New Hope Baptist Church could only envision providing quality service for families if the service is local. Quality family service for families in need and local service are, to a large extent, interchangeable.

> It's ingrained in us; it's who we are. We could have placed our site anywhere. Families *with means* are able to do what they need to do to get their children to the best facilities. We chose to create the best facilities right where families *without means* would still be able to participate. Our success has been that we've been able to truly serve the families and children that have the greatest need.

For New Hope Baptist Church, there can be no services for neighborhood families without using the neighborhood.

Along with valuing the capacity for success of the people in the neighborhood, safety was another reason to provide education for the children right in their own community. "This is where they feel safe. Why take that person out of their safety zone?" questions Deisy Madrigal. It was simple. "We wanted to help our community, so we needed to find a location where they [in the community] felt safe and secure." Common sense and logic make clear that services for families in need are really only services if they are nearby. Familiarity often breeds feelings of safety for communities that may have historically been made to feel that they have to go far beyond their community walls for livelihood opportunities.

Kathy Brower, former head of SECOM Ministries, agrees. "You can't do anything with people if they don't feel safe, if they can't trust you." Safety and trust were built by locating the educational resources right in their family's own neighborhoods, in collaboration with organizations they already knew and trusted. Children were not being loaded onto buses and carried across town to be with strangers all day. They were just down the street with neighbors and friends. To no surprise, being neighborly and friendly yields positive outcomes. "They make you feel like a family," relays Brenda, a parent with ELNC. "[My son] gives them all hugs first thing when he gets there." Ebony, another parent, recognizes that family feeling as well. "[It's] Like I'm walking into one of my aunt's homes or my grandma's house." "Everyone takes the time to get to know you."

Ebony continues: "Going to school shouldn't be a burden." Ebony is correct. Placing classrooms in the neighborhood removes the burden from parents to provide transportation and other resources that parents may not have for quality ECE. "It became the neighborhood heartbeat," according to Sharon Killebrew. "Everything about it was theirs." Local ownership of neighborhood resources, says Killebrew, is key.

Two generation

Creating opportunities for and addressing needs of both vulnerable children and their parents together is the focus.

Similar to the United States federally funded pre-K program Headstart (Duch, 2005; Manz, 2012), ELNC has adopted a two-generation approach to early learning. ELNC understands the importance of a parent in a child's educational success. Such may sound like what other educational programs claim. But at ELNC, programming for parents is a normative operational value. Ownership of learning of the neighborhood's children belongs to the neighborhood because ELNC values place-based education. Parents are the "first teacher" for a child, explains Ezeh. The school teacher is the second teacher, and environment that includes the larger neighborhood is the third teacher (Lara-Cinisomo et al., 2007). This order foregrounds parents above all others as the child's teacher and reminds parents of their own role as the leader in their child's education. This order of teachers as second in command offers humility to all stakeholders involved in a child's learning and empowers parents who know their children best.

Parental input and involvement are invaluable.

> "The parents are our customers—they're the drivers," exclaims Killebrew. "When we say we want parents to be the drivers of their children's education, but then we tell them how to drive, it's not going to work. You have to honor and allow that family to develop their own strategies, be there to support and coach, and provide feedback, but in the end they need to own it. That's the only permanent, sustainable change there will be—is if they own it. And that's what ELNC does: it opens up possibilities for them."

ELNC understands well that any services provided for children can really only be sustained with the leadership of parents. Four-year olds are not independent learners. They need 24-hour guidance and supervision in and outside of the classroom. The only sure way for whatever learning they experience at the little school or *La Escuelita* to register is with modeling and reinforcements from their parents.

ELNC centers parental rights, focusing on parents owning their role as the "project manager" of their child's educational success. "We are working to put parents in the driver's seat, empowered to direct their child's success," maintains Ezeh. "And to do that they need to be able to see all of it." Devising a system of parent teachers, family coaches, and other ways for parents to be the drivers of their children's education creates the conditions for parents to have their eyes on critical aspects of the EPIC ELNC experience.

The EPIC (Empower Parents Impacting Children) model provided not only training and resources to parents, which has connected them to job opportunities and other basic necessities. In addition, the model asks parents to advocate for their children, even in political advocacy efforts at the state level. Parents hold their own power. They elect themselves to executive positions of the learning of their children. ELNC staff and other stakeholders learn from parents how to educate.

> Many practitioners in early childhood go into it because they are passionate about little children—they love little kids. They have a way with children; they're comfortable in that space. Nkechy has all of that but what she's passionate about is the parents, explains Dana Boals.
>
> As much as the programs have good curriculum and teachers in the classroom, there needs to be more than just classroom curriculum. At ELNC, we have researched based curriculum, quality classrooms with wonderful teachers.

Parents mold and shape their children at home. In a typical early childhood classroom, teachers may try to figure out how to educate children without even at times conferencing with parents (Gross et al., 2020). ELNC's paradigm leans into knowledge of the parents to create knowledge from students. From Ezeh's perspective "If we pour everything into the child and don't pour into the parents and the family, we're doing them a disservice. And our efforts will not be sustainable."

The ELNC model is based on core, primary values of outcomes, cultural competence, creativity and innovation, place-based, and two-generation operations. Staff and stakeholders believe in, recite, implement these values to carry out the organizational mission so that early childhood is a quality equitable experience for those that have historically not received their fair share of educational equity.

References

Alexandersen, N., Zachrisson, H. D., Wilhelmsen, T., Wang, M. V., & Brandlistuen, R. E. (2021). Predicting selection into ECEC of higher quality in a universal context: The role of parental education and income. *Early Childhood Research Quarterly*, *55*, 336–348.

Allen-Handy, A., & Farinde-Wu, A. (2017). Reflecting back while gazing forward: Black female teachers and the diversification of the United States' teacher workforce. In A. Farinde-Wu, A. Allen-Handy, & C. W. Lewis (Eds.), *Black female teachers*. Bingley: Emerald Publishing Limited.

Arndt, S. (2018). Early childhood teacher cultural otherness and belonging. *Contemporary Issues in Early Childhood*, *19*(4), 392–403.

Arthur, L., Beecher, B., Death, E., Dockett, S., & Farmer, S. (2017). *Programming and planning in early childhood settings*. Cengage Australia.

Barnett, W. S. (2010). Universal and targeted approaches to preschool education in the United States. *International Journal of Child Care and Education Policy*, *4*(1), 1–12.

Bergroth, M., & Palviainen, Å. (2016). The early childhood education and care partnership for bilingualism in minority language schooling: Collaboration between bilingual families and pedagogical practitioners. *International Journal of Bilingual Education and Bilingualism*, *19*(6), 649–667.

Bigras, N. (2010). A comparative study of structural and process quality in center-based and family-based child care services. *Child & Youth Care Forum*, *39*(9), 129–150.

Cleveland, G., Corter, C., Pelletier, J., Colley, S., Bertrand, J., & Jamieson, J. (2006). *A review of the state of the field of early childhood learning and development in child care, kindergarten and family support programs*. Toronto, Ontario: Atkinson Centre for Society and Child Development, Ontario Institute for Studies in Education, University of Toronto. Retrieved from https://www. ccl-cca.ca/NR/rdonlyres/67F194AF-8EB5-487D-993C-7CF9B565DDB3/0/SFREarlyChildhoodLearning.pdf

Cloney, D., Cleveland, G., Hattie, J., & Tayler, C. (2016). Variations in the availability and quality of early childhood education and care by socioeconomic status of neighborhoods. *Early Education and Development*, *27*(3), 384–401.

Cumming, T., Sumsion, J., & Wong, S. (2015). Early childhood practice and refrains of complexity. *Early Years*, *35*(1), 80–95.

Cycyk, L. M., & Hammer, C. S. (2020). Beliefs, values, and practices of Mexican immigrant families towards language and learning in toddlerhood: Setting the foundation for early childhood education. *Early Childhood Research Quarterly*, *52*, 25–37.

Deedy, C. A., & Austin, M. (2014, March 1). *Martina the beautiful cockroach: A Cuban Folktale* (Turtleback Binding Edition). St. Louis, MO: Turtleback.

Duch, H. (2005). Redefining parent involvement in Head Start: A two-generation approach. *Early Child Development and Care*, *175*(1), 23–35.

Echevarria, J., Vogt, M., & Short, D. J. (2017). *Making content comprehensible for English learners: The SIOP model* (5th ed.). New York, NY: Pearson.

Einarsdottir, J., & Jónsdóttir, A. H. (2019). Parent-preschool partnership: Many levels of power. *Early Years*, *39*(2), 175–189.

Garrity, S. M., Longstreth, S. L., Lazarevic, V., & Black, F. (2021, March). Examining the tensions between cultural models of care in family childcare and quality rating improvement systems. *Children and Youth Services Review*, *122*, 105927.

Gross, D., Bettencourt, A. F., Taylor, K., Francis, L., Bower, K., & Singleton, D. L. (2020). What is parent engagement in early learning? Depends who you ask. *Journal of Child and Family Studies*, *29*(3), 747–760.

Halgunseth, L. (2009). Family engagement, diverse families, and early childhood. *Young Children*, *64*(5), 56–58.

Hnasko, A. (2020). The work of early childhood coaches in one US state. *International Journal of Mentoring and Coaching in Education*, *9*(2), 137–152.

Horm, D. M., Yazejian, N., Kennel, P., & Jackson, C. (2017). Educare: A model for US early childhood services. In L. Miller, C. Cameron, C. Dalli, & N. Barbour (Eds.), *The SAGE handbook of early childhood policy*. Chicago, IL: SAGE Publications.

Hyman, T. S. (1983, January 1). *Little red riding hood* (reprint). Kutahya: Kura Publishing House.

Infurna, C. J. (2020). What makes a great preschool teacher? Best practices and classroom quality in an urban early childhood setting. *International Electronic Journal of Elementary Education, 13*(2), 227–239.

Iruka, I. U., Gardner-Neblett, N., Telfer, N. A., Ibekwe-Okafor, N., Curenton, S. M., Sims, J., Sansbury, A. B., & Neblett, E. W. (2022). Effects of racism on child development: Advancing ant-racist developmental science. *Annual Review for Developmental Psychology, 4*, 109–132.

Jayaraman, G., Marvin, C., Knoche, L., & Bainter, S. (2015). Coaching conversations in early childhood programs. *Infants & Young Children, 28*(4), 323–336.

Jeon, S., Choi, J. Y., Horm, D. M., & Castle, S. (2018, October). Early Head Start dosage: The role of parent-caregiver relationships and family involvement. *Children and Youth Services Review, 93*, 291–300.

Jose, K., Taylor, C. L., Jones, R., Banks, S., Stafford, J., Zubrick, S. R., Stubbs, M., Preen, D. B., Venn, A., & Hansen, E. (2021). The impact on service collaboration of co-location of early childhood services in Tasmanian child and family centres: An ethnographic study. *International journal of integrated care, 21*(2), 1–13.

Keller, T., & Franzak, J. K. (2016). When names and schools collide: Critically analyzing depictions of culturally and linguistically diverse children negotiating their names in picture books. *Children's Literature in Education, 47*(2), 177–190.

King, D. (2010). Learning by listening: Emotional reflexivity and organizational change in childcare. In *Emotionalizing organizations and organizing emotions* (pp. 230–250). Palgrave Macmillan, London.

Kocyigit, S. (2015). Family involvement in preschool education: Rationale, problems and solutions for the participants. *Educational Sciences: Theory & Practice, 15*(1), 141–157.

Lara-Cinisomo, S., Fuligni, A. S., Ritchie, S., Howes, C., & Karoly, L. (2007, October 25). Getting ready for school: An examination of early childhood educators' belief systems. *Early Childhood Education Journal*, *35*(4), 343–349. https://doi.org/10.1007/s10643-007-0215-2

Lee, B. Y. (2013). Heritage language maintenance and cultural identity formation: The case of Korean immigrant parents and their children in the USA. *Early Child Development and Care*, *183*(11), 1576–1588.

Lenhoff, S. W., Singer, J., Stokes, K., Mahowald, J. B., & Khawaja, S. (2022). Beyond the bus: Reconceptualizing school transportation for mobility justice. *Harvard Educational Review*, *92*(3), 336–360.

Leverett, L. (2006, September 5). Closing the achievement gap: "All children can learn". *Edutopia*. Retrieved September 5, 2006 from https://www.edutopia.org/closing-achievement-gap

Lino, D. (2016). Early childhood education: Key competences in teacher education. *Educația Plus*, *14*(3), 7–15.

Lungu, S., Matafwali, B., & Banja, M. K. (2021). Formative and summative assessment practices by teachers in early childhood education centres in Lusaka, Zambia. *European Journal of Education Studies*, *8*(2), e3549.

Manz, P. (2012, March 18). Home-based head start and family involvement: An exploratory study of the associations among home visiting frequency and family involvement dimensions. *Early Childhood Education Journal*, *40*(4), 231–238.

Mawas, N., & Muntean, C. H. (2018). *Supporting lifelong learning through development of 21st century skills*. 10th International Conference on Education and New Learning Technologies, pp. 7343–7350. Dublin: National College of Ireland.

McCarthy, L., Delbosc, A., Currie, G., & Molloy, A. (2017). Factors influencing travel mode choice among families with young children (aged 0–4): A review of the literature. *Transport Reviews*, *37*(6), 767–781.

McDermott, G. (1987, March 15). *Anansi the spider: A tale from the Ashanti* (1st ed.). New York, NY: Henry Holt and Company.

McLaughlin, D. V. (2020). Partner with parents: Best practices for building strong parent collaboration. In *Personalized principal leadership practices* (pp. 167–192). Emerald Publishing Limited, Bingley.

Moore, L. L., Slanda, D. D., Placencia, A., & Moore, M. M. (2020). The power of a name: Nontraditional names, teacher efficacy, and expected learning outcomes. *Journal of English Learner Education*, *11*(1), 83–103.

Moreno, G., & Gaytán, F. X. (2013). Focus on Latino learners: Developing a foundational understanding of Latino cultures to cultivate student success. *Preventing School Failure: Alternative Education for Children and Youth*, *57*(1), 7–16.

Pacchiano, D. M., Wagner, M. R., Lewandowski, H., Ehrlich, S. B., & Stein, A. G. (2018). *Early education essentials: Illustrations of strong organizational practices in programs poised for improvement*. Chicago: The Ounce of Prevention Fund and the University of Chicago Consortium on School Research.

Page, J., & Eadie, P. (2019). Coaching for continuous improvement in collaborative, interdisciplinary early childhood teams. *Australasian Journal of Early Childhood*, *44*(3), 270–284.

Pasini, N. (2018). A collective impact approach to the reading achievement gap. *Journal of Library Administration*, *58*(6), 605–616.

Porterfield, M. L., & Scott-Little, C. (2019). Policy levers to promote cultural competence in early childhood programs in the USA: Recommendations from system specialists. *International Journal of Child Care and Education Policy*, *13*(1), 1–23.

Powell, D. (1998). Reweaving parents into the fabric of early childhood programs. *Young Children*, *53*(5), 60–67.

Rasheed, D. S., Brown, J. L., Doyle, S. L., & Jennings, P. A. (2019, June 23). The effect of teacher–child race/ethnicity matching and classroom diversity on children's socioemotional and academic skills. *Child Development*, *91*(3), e597–e618.

Raynal, A., Lavigne, H., Goldstein, M., & Gutierrez, J. (2021, May 30). Starting with parents: Investigating a multi-generational, media-enhanced approach to support informal science learning for young children. *Early Childhood Education Journal*, *50*(5), 879–889.

Salminen, J. (2017). Early childhood education and care system in Finland. *Nauki o Wychowaniu. Studia Interdyscyplinarne*, *5*(2), 135–154.

Carolyn Sattin-Bajaj, 2023. "Student Transportation in Choice-Rich Districts: Implementation Challenges and Responses," *Education Finance and Policy*, MIT Press, vol. 18(2), pages 351–364, Spring.

Shannon, S. M. (2010). The debate on bilingual education in the US: Language ideology as reflected in the practice of bilingual teachers. *Language Ideological Debates*, *2*, 171–199.

Sinclair, K. (2021). Disrupting normalised discourses: Ways of knowing, being and doing cultural competence. *The Australian Journal of Indigenous Education*, *50*(1), 203–211.

Sullivan, D. (2016). *Cultivating the genius of Black children: Strategies to close the achievement gap in the early years*. St. Paul, MN: Redleaf Press.

Trapani, I. (1998, September 1). *The Itsy Bitsy Spider (Iza Trapani's extended nursery rhymes)* (Board Book). StreetWatertown, MA: Charlesbridge.

van Oers, B. (2013). Educational innovation between freedom and fixation: The cultural-political construction of innovations in early childhood education in the Netherlands. *International Journal of Early Years Education*, *21*(2–3), 178–191.

Varshney, N., Lee, S., Temple, J. A., & Reynolds, A. J. (2020, October). Does early childhood education enhance parental school involvement in second grade? Evidence from Midwest Child-Parent Center Program. *Children and Youth Services Review*, *117*, 105317.

Vesely, C. K., Ewaida, M., & Anderson, E. A. (2014). Cultural competence of parenting education programs used by Latino families: A review. *Hispanic Journal of Behavioral Sciences*, *36*(1), 27–47.

West-Olatunji, C. A., Behar-Horenstein, L., Rant, J., & Cohen-Phillips, L. N. (2008). Enhancing cultural competence among teachers of African American children using mediated lesson study. *The Journal of Negro Education*, *77*(1), 27–38.

Worthington, M., & van Oers, B. (2017). Children's social literacies: Meaning making and the emergence of graphical signs and texts in pretence. *Journal of Early Childhood Literacy*, *17*(2), 147–175.

5

What is child development?

For over 50 years, Ezeh has been involved in all aspects of child development: first, as a child herself growing up in her village in the state of Enugu in Nigeria; second, as an adult mother developing her own children in the city of Grand Rapids, Michigan; third, as a teacher instructing children from birth to age eight; eventually, as a college professor educating others on how to develop their Early Childhood Education (ECE) skills; into serving as a consultant around the globe helping communities emerge with culturally competent early childhood curriculum; and ultimately, as an advocate developing and improving policies for children in communities historically written off by society.

One of the big questions for those with interest in ELNC as an organization is what is child development and how does ELNC's definition of child development shape educator practice? How does Ezeh, staff, and collaborative partners of ELNC define child development? To what extent, based on ELNC conceptions of child development, does ELNC engage in developmentally appropriate practice (Bredekamp, 1986, 1987)? Textbooks will tell you that child development refers to the sequence of physical, language, thought, and emotional changes that occur in a child from birth to the beginning of adulthood. During this process, a child progresses from dependency on their parents/guardians or community members to increasing independence. Child development is strongly influenced by genetic factors and events during prenatal life and by environmental facts and the child's learning capacity. Logically, one may start with a temporal view of child development, which is the period from when a child exits the mother's womb until the beginning of teenage hood. This textbook definition also includes a developmental framework of child development that can be described as the stages from birth to adolescence. ELNC has grown the institution based on both perspectives and also, because the organization is led by an expert in ECE who has been informed by various child development theories.

For years, social scientists have studied children and provided insight into what occurs neurologically, behaviorally, and physically. Various theories associated with child development have arisen from these insights. Chief among those theories include the following:

- Sigmund Freud (1923) declares that behavior is controlled by unconscious urges and heavily colored by emotion. He proposed that personality has three structures: id, ego, and super ego.
- John Watson (1913) and Ivan Pavlov (1927) maintain that all human behavior is observable behavior that can be learned through experience with the environment.
- BF Skinner (1938) emphasized that development consists of patterns of behavioral change that are brought about by rewards, punishments, or reinforcement.
- BF Skinner described in terms of environmental influences; such a theory is premised on learning taking place purely through processes of association and reinforcement.
- Arnold Gesell (1925) was a "maturationist." Gesell's maturationist approach centers on the belief that growth and development happen orderly in stages and sequence and that the individual genetic timetable affects rate of maturation.
- Jean Piaget (1957) and Lev Vygotsky (1978) were cognitive theorists who were concerned with the development of a person's thought process. These thought processes influence how children understand and interact with the world.

- Vygotsky portrayed the child's development as inseparable from social and cultural activities.
- Erik Erikson (1950, 1968, 1982) championed a psychosocial theory that focused on development across the entire lifespan. At each stage, according to Erikson, children and adults face a developmental crisis that serves as a major turning point in their lives. Successfully managing the challenges of each stage leads to the emergence of a lifelong psychological virtue.
- John Bowlby (1969, 1988) stresses that infants and their primary caregivers are biologically predisposed to form attachment to each other. The newborn is biologically equipped to elicit attachment behavior. It suggests that children are born with an innate need to form attachments and that such attachments aid in survival by ensuring that the child receives care and protection.
- Albert Bandura's (1977) "social learning theory is learning that occurs through observing what others do." So, it speaks to a view that behaviors can be learned through observation and modeling. For example, by observing the actions of others, including parents and peers, children develop new skills and acquire new information.
- Information processing theory which emphasizes that individuals manipulate information, monitor it, and strategize about it. Information processing focuses on innate learning ability. Children are born with specialized information-processing abilities that enable them to become aware of and act upon their own development.
- Uri Bronfenbrenner's (1979) ecological theory suggests that there is a balance between nature and nurture. He argued that each child is placed in the middle of concentric factors that influence the child. Emphasis is placed both on environment and heredity.
- Jeanne Chall's (1983) developmental theories on reading/literacy stem mostly from her work with first graders. Chall posited that there are six stages of reading, with the first three labeled as learning to read. Logically, the last

three are called reading to learn. United States programs and policies are designed for learners to be independent readers by the end of the third grade, which roughly signals the end of learning to read stages. Children in early childhood, particularly children ages 4–5 whom ELNC serves, are at stage 0 of Chall's child development design that she has dubbed pre-reading; they acquire language from their parents or other family members that become the basis for reading in preschool or in kindergarten.

Child development does not occur in isolation, despite these distinct theories and stages of child development. In other words, from the perspective of ELNC, there is no one theory that accounts for the complexity of how a child develops. Good early childhood educators and programs know that a range of theories of early childhood are employed to address the individual and collective needs of children. Each of the theories described above are necessary perspectives to solve child development problems; they help educators to approach children's needs from different angles. An integrated and eclectic approach remains the default for ELNC design of quality early childhood programs.

As aforementioned, Ezeh's motivation to study child development – and to later focus on ECE – stems from her becoming a mother. The birth of her first child, Onyinyé MK, now an attorney, was the catalyst. ECE offered practical knowledge on how to educate her child. Early childhood education is a broad term used to describe any type of educational program that serves children in their preschool years, before they are old enough to enter kindergarten or primary school (Auld & Morris, 2019). Beyond acquiring knowledge on how to best care for her new child, Ezeh pursued ECE as a means to continue her own post-secondary education. No doubt, the absence of her traditional family support system close by meant that she had to find alternative ways to raise her children. But the opportunity to pursue advanced degrees could not be ignored.

ECE study throughout college afforded Ezeh the opportunity to deeply explore the many theories of child development mentioned above. Her children, with four more following

Onyinyé MK, became her laboratory subjects (McBride et al., 2012). Ezeh was able to test theories of child development with them, based on more direct observation than any laboratory could provide (McBride et al., 2012). Testing these theories with her own children was important to offset absent or negative representation in her children's school curricula. Many textbooks, peer students, and teachers of her children were not racially, ethnically, or culturally diverse. Like many Black kids schooling in the United States (Yoon & Templeton, 2022), Ezeh's children had few opportunities to see themselves in what they read, with whom they interacted, and by whom they were being taught.

Ezeh's mentor, the late Professor Janice Hale Benson, and A. G. Hilliard (1986), published a book called *Black Children: Their Roots, Culture, and Learning Styles*. This publication became Ezeh's ECE bible early in her career, helping Ezeh confirm what she knew about children: that they are born with the potential to learn, that they are very resilient, and – when given a nurturing environment – can reach maximum potential.

Professor Hale and her Early Childhood Education program "Visions for Children" fueled Ezeh's motherhood passion. Ezeh also had the example of her own father's treatment of her and her siblings (Ezeh, 2020). Both of these life experiences provided examples for how Ezeh could best understand child development and subsequently advocate for vulnerable children.

Ostensibly, understanding and valuing the whole child mandates deep knowledge of child development. Child development theories and basic humanist understanding provide educators with insight into each child's unique cognitive, emotional, physical, social, and educational needs from birth right into early adulthood.

But Ezeh will also be the first to say that parents do not need to be experts on the theories of child development to do a good job of raising their child; they just need to be interested in and supportive of their child's learning (Pattison et al., 2022). "Everyday parents don't need to read a 50-year-old book by Piaget on how to create a stimulating environment for your child," she laughs. Child development in its simple form, according to Ezeh, is knowing how to use ordinary moments and everyday routines to promote a child's development at appropriate stages. "At every given stage, a child is growing and developing, and each stage brings its own challenges and opportunities," she explains. "Part of early childhood education is knowing what stage the child is in so you can take advantage of that stage, helping a child reach their highest potential." By taking advantage of that stage, Ezeh means zeroing in on the particularities of socio-emotional, neurological, and other forms of development (Smith & Glass, 2019). Obviously, what a child needs at one year of age is different from his or her needs at age 4 (World Health Organization, 2018).

In particular, what one may refer to as "kindergarten readiness" (Kagan & Rigby, 2003; Ready at Five, 2020) is a way to measure development. However, children need more than learning or cognitive development to be "kindergarten ready" (Duncan et al., 2007). In fact, there are four separate areas of development for school readiness: physical, cognitive, social, and emotional (Kagan & Rigby, 2003; Smith & Glass, 2019; Welsh et al., 2010). "Sometimes social and emotional development is combined, and that's when we get in trouble," warns Ezeh. "Because we don't pay attention to the emotional part. We pay attention to the social part." What Ezeh is referring to as "social" is the extent to which and types of interactions a child has with other children and even teachers in the classroom (Welsh et al., 2010). On the other hand, "emotional" indicates the expressions, feelings, and responses to social interactions in a child's environment at home and school as well as other life circumstances including perhaps such mundane things as the weather (Denham et al., 2012).

While emotional development often takes a back seat to social development, there are dangers to focusing on the emotional aspects of a child (Weiland & Yoshikawa, 2013). Too often, any focus on emotional development looks more like controlling, or shutting down, emotions. "We shut down the emotional part and concentrate on the social. Yes, I need to know how to behave in a social context, how to behave when I'm out there, but this comes with age," Ezeh explains. Kindergarten readiness, then, is when a child is on track in all four areas of development – *and* the child is self-assured, with a sense of knowing who he or she is to the point of including but not limited to executive functioning (Burchinal et al., 2023). "If socially and emotionally a child is not on target, they are not ready for kindergarten," Ezeh asserts.

> Without social and emotional development, a child is not going to be happy deep down. When a child is on target for all of this, believe it or not, the reading, the writing—everything comes out. Everything else develops along with it.

Cognitive development, according to Ezeh, can be best developed when children are healthy and developing socially and emotionally (Welsh et al., 2010). As previously stated, these are components of a larger child development whole. Because the various components are interconnected, one cannot ignore one part of child development without ignoring another part. Physical development of the child, for instance, has an impact on cognitive development of the child (National Association for the Education of Young Children [NAEYC], 2022).

Ezeh knew these truths about developing the whole child from her experience as a mother, her studies, and observing her father raise her and her siblings in their village in Nigeria (Ezeh, 2020). Nonetheless, her service as the Director of REACH Child Care Center, a nonprofit organization serving vulnerable children in Grand Rapids, Michigan, offered the most clarity on the utility of each theory of child development. Ezeh's professional experience as Director of REACH Child Care Center gave her applied understanding of the conceptual knowledge about how children develop. The theories she was learning in school were now active, real. The social, physical, and cognitive development of a child is *negatively* impacted when an environment of poverty surrounds them during their prenatal experience through early childhood (World Health Organization, 2018). Expertise in all of these areas of development is required for educators to really educate each child (NAEYC, 2022).

While some students of child development specialize in one theory or another, Ezeh seeks a holistic approach (Albarran, 2014; Salminen, 2017) that she adds to her unorthodox beliefs about child development. Ezeh holds to a strong belief in Bronfenbrenner's ecological theory that suggests that a child is placed in the middle of influential concentric factors (Bronfenbrenner, 1979). With Bronfenbrenner, emphasis is placed *both* on environment and heredity. It is the classic nature and nurture stance in social science to which Ezeh attributes her theoretical and empirical views on educating children. Ezeh supports Vygotsky's theory as well, a theory that sees children not as solitary discoverers of knowledge but as learners within cultural and social interactions. Vygotsky (1978) also emphasized the role of language in the development of thinking processes as verbal and non-verbal language communication supporting child growth in part by revealing to adults what children know or not. Such a theory also provides direction to where children should be led.

As a former teacher, Ezeh spent many days in the classroom, specifically with vulnerable children. Ezeh's teaching experience helped her tremendously to gain valuable insight into the practical implementation of child development and associated learning theories. As a Professor of Early Childhood Education who prepares new teachers, she is also able to draw upon perspectives gained through her direct involvement in the community of the children she serves. Ezeh has learned that while she prepares preschool teachers to teach all children, she must also ensure that vulnerable children are ready to learn (Dalziel et al., 2015).

These practical, professional experiences have continued to fuel Ezeh's passion for advocating for quality early learning opportunities for vulnerable children. Her lived experiences in Nigeria to Michigan, involvement in community programs with families, and the various child development and educational theories have guided her over the years to become the foundational framework that anchors the work of the Early Learning Neighborhood Collaborative (ELNC)'s two-generational approach to ECE.

ELNC's work is critical to the development of children in Grand Rapids, Michigan, and beyond (Miller, 2021; Scott, 2016; Stukkie, 2012). Every ELNC classroom places children at the center with their parents and teachers working together to support children to reach their potential (Adams & McDaniel, 2009). ELNC acts as an interface between the micro-system of families living within hyper-localized communities and the macro-systemic level of ECE (Bar-On, 2004; Diamond-Berry & Ezeh, 2020; Kay, 2022; Mok & Morris, 2012; U.S. Department of Education, 2018).

In short, the use of child development theories at ELNC is predicated on ELNC commitment to producing outcomes that further the following core ELNC beliefs:

- Every child deserves a fair chance at success in school and life.
- The economic security of families is crucial to creating the optimal conditions through which children can develop, learn, and grow.
- People have the inherent capacity to solve their own problems and social transformation is within the reach of all communities.
- Racial healing and racial equity are essential to accomplish a mission of creating conditions in which vulnerable children can succeed.

These core beliefs can be viewed as ELNC's model that employs a "Hub and Spoke" delivery system of quality ECE services. These services include *place-based* strategies, programs that are embedded in the institutions of trust in the community so that children are surrounded by culturally relevant environments, two-generational family engagement, and indigenous (Ezeh, 2022) community leadership development. ELNC believes successful child development results from cooperation with the communities of the child. Each child must be provided for with sufficient resources and necessary tools and have the inherent capacity to solve their own problems. Moreover, the child's entire community of parents, teachers, and other adult figures can be transformed using equity initiatives.

References

Adams, G., & McDaniel, M. (2009). *Fulfilling the Promise of Preschool for All: Insights into Issues Affecting Access for Selected Immigrant Groups in Chicago.* Washington, DC: The Urban Institute.

Albarran, A. S. (2014). *Improving school readiness through parent education programming: Understanding the role of community-based organizations in a large urban city center.* ProQuest LLC, Ann Arbor, MI.

Auld, E., & Morris, P. (2019). The OECD and IELS: Redefining early childhood education for the 21st century. *Policy Futures in Education, 17*(1), 11–26.

Bandura, A. (1977). *Social learning theory.* Englewood Cliffs, NJ: Prentice Hall.

Bar-On, A. (2004, February). Early childhood care and education in Africa. *Journal of Early Childhood Research, 2*(1), 67–84. https://doi.org/10.1177/1476718x0421004

Bowlby, J. (1969). *Attachment and loss, Vol. 1: Attachment.* New York, NY: Basic Books.

Bowlby, J. (1988). Attachment, communication, and the therapeutic process. In *A secure base: Parent-child attachment and healthy human development* (pp. 137–157). Milton Park: Taylor & Francis Group.

Bredekamp, S. (Ed.). (1986). *Developmentally appropriate practice.* Washington, DC: NAEYC.

Bredekamp, S. (1987). *Developmentally appropriate practice in early childhood Programs serving children from birth through age 8.* Washington, DC: NAEYC.

Bronfenbrenner, U. (1979). *The ecology of human development.* New York, NY: Harvard University Press.

Burchinal, M., Pianta, R., Ansari, A., Whittaker, J., & Vitiello, V. (2023). Kindergarten academic and social skills and exposure to peers with pre-kindergarten experience. *Early Childhood Research Quarterly, 62*, 41–52.

Chall, J. S. (1983). *Stages of reading development.* New York, NY: McGraw-Hill.

Dalziel, K. M., Halliday, D., & Segal, L. (2015, February 17). Assessment of the cost–benefit literature on early childhood education for vulnerable children. *SAGE Open*, *5*(1). https://doi.org/10.1177/2158244015571637

Denham, S. A., Bassett, H. H., & Zinsser, K. (2012). Early childhood teachers as socializers of young children's emotional competence. *Early Childhood Education Journal*, *40*(3), 137–143.

Diamond-Berry, K., & Ezeh, N. (2020). Early learning neighborhood collaborative: Hidden in plain view. *Zero to Three*, *41*(1), 13–20.

Duncan, G. J., Dowsett, C. J., Claessens, A., Magnuson, K., Huston, A. C., Klebanov, P., Pagani, L. S., Feinstein, L., Engel, M., Brooks-Gunn, J., Sexton, H., Duckworth, K., & Japel, C. (2007). School readiness and later achievement. *Developmental Psychology*, *43*, 1428–1446.

Erikson, E. H. (1950). *Childhood and society*. New York, NY: W. W. Norton & Co.

Erikson, E. H. (1968). *Identity: Youth and crisis*. New York, NY: Norton & Co.

Erikson, E. H. (1982). *The life cycle completed*. New York, NY: Norton.

Ezeh, N. (2020). *Nwaenyi: Child of an elephant: Lessons learned from my father, a Nigerian chief, about child development and affirmations* [Independently published].

Ezeh, N. (2022). *Leading while learning* [Unpublished manuscript].

Freud, S. (1923). The ego and the id. In J. Strachey (Trans.), *The standard edition of the complete psychological works of Sigmund Freud* (Vol. XIX). London: Hogarth Press.

Gesell, A. (1925). *The mental growth of the pre-school child: A psychological outline of normal development from birth to the sixth year, including a system of developmental diagnosis*. New York, NY: Macmillan.

Hale-Benson, J. E., & Hilliard, A. G., III. (1986). *Black children: Their roots, culture, and learning styles* (Revised). Baltimore, MD: Johns Hopkins University Press.

Kagan, S. L., & Rigby, E. (2003). *Improving the readiness of children for school: Recommendations for state policy*. Washington, DC: Center for the Study of Social Policy.

Kay, L. (2022). 'What works' and for whom? Bold Beginnings and the construction of the school ready child. *Journal of Early Childhood Research*, *20*(2), 172–184.

McBride, B. A., Groves, M., Barbour, N., Horm, D., Stremmel, A., Lash, M., Bersani, C., Ratekin, C., Moran, J., Elicker, J., & Toussaint, S. (2012). Child development laboratory schools as generators of knowledge in early childhood education: New models and approaches. *Early Education & Development, 23*(2), 153–164.

Miller, K. (2021). *$12.4M grant aimed at expanding early education to Kalamazoo's underserved children*. Mlive. Retrieved September 27, 2022, from https://www.mlive.com/news/kalamazoo/2021/12/124m-grant-aimed-at-expanding-early-education-to-kalamazoos-underserved-children.html

Mok, A., & Morris, M. W. (2012). Managing two cultural identities: The malleability of bicultural identity integration as a function of induced global or local processing. *Personality and Social Psychology Bulletin, 38*(2), 233–246.

National Association for the Education of Young Children. (2022). *Principles of child development and learning and implications that inform practice*. Retrieved October 15, 2022, from https://www.naeyc.org/resources/position-statements/dap/principles

Pattison, S., Ramos Montañez, S., & Svarovsky, G. (2022). *Family values, parent roles, and life challenges: Parent reflections on the factors shaping long-term interest development for young children and their families participating in an early childhood engineering program*. Science Education. https://doi.org/10.1002/sce.21763

Pavlov, I. P. (1927). *Conditioned reflexes: An investigation of the physiological activity of the cerebral cortex*. Cambridge, MA: Oxford University Press.

Piaget, J. (1957). *Construction of reality in the child*. London: Routledge & Kegan Paul. Ready at Five. (2020). Readiness matters: 2019–2020 kindergarten readiness assessment report. Retrieved from https://earlychildhood.marylandpublicschools.org/system/files/filedepot/4/200178_ready5_book_web.pdf

Salminen, J. (2017). Early childhood education and care system in Finland. *Nauki o Wychowaniu. Studia Interdyscyplinarne, 5*(2), 135–154.

Scott, M. (2016, February 16). *Second $5M grant awarded to early learning effort in Grand Rapids*. Mlive. Retrieved September 30, 2022, from https://www.mlive.com/news/grand-rapids/2016/02/wk_kellogg_foundation_awards_5.html

Skinner, B. F. (1938). *The behavior of organisms: an experimental analysis*. London: Sage Publication.

Smith, N., & Glass, W. (2019). Ready or not? Teachers' perceptions of young children's school readiness. *Journal of Early Childhood Research, 17*(4), 329–346.

Stukkie, H. (2012). Early learning neighborhood collaborative prepares children for kindergarten and life. *Rapid Growth*. Retrieved October 15, 2022, from https://www.rapidgrowthmedia.com/features/11082012early.aspx

U.S. Department of Education. (2018). *Improving basic programs operated by local educational agencies (Title I, Part A)*. https://www2.ed.gov/programs/titleiparta/index.html

Vygotsky, L. S. (1978). *Mind in society: The development of higher psychological processes*. Cambridge, MA: Harvard University Press.

Watson, J. B. (1913). Psychology as the behaviorist views it. *Psychological Review, 20*(2), 158–177.

Weiland, C., & Yoshikawa, H. (2013). Impacts of a prekindergarten program on children's mathematics, language, literacy, executive function, and emotional skills. *Child Development, 84*(6), 2112–2130.

Welsh, J. A., Nix, R. L., Blair, C., Bierman, K. L., & Nelson, K. E. (2010). The development of cognitive skills and gains in academic school readiness for children from low-income families. *Journal of Educational Psychology, 102*(1), 43–53. https://doi.org/10.1037/a0016738

World Health Organization. (2018). *Nurturing care for early childhood development: A framework for helping children survive and thrive to transform health and human potential*. Geneva: World Health Organization.

Yoon, H. S., & Templeton, T. N. (2022). Reflecting, representing, and expanding the narrative (s) in early childhood curriculum. *Urban Education*. https://doi.org/10.1177/00420859221097893

6

Guiding principles
What ELNC believes about children

Education programs are driven by people who hold certain principles about learners and learning. Chapter 5 revealed that Early Learning Neighborhood Collaborative (ELNC) is anchored in a multifaceted, holistic approach to child development. One theory does not fit all children. Instead, multiple, and perhaps divergent, theories often fit each child (Odom, 2016). Chapter 4 discussed the values of ELNC. Beyond a strong theoretical foundation of child development and values ELNC embedded into operations, there are associated principles that must undergird ELNC programs. Those who staff and run education programs enact principles based on what they know about those on the receiving end of programming efforts (Lara-Cinisomo et al., 2007). The National Association for the Education of Young Children (NAEYC) offers "…nine principles and their implications for early childhood education professional practice" (NAEYC, 2022). The quality of targeted education services reveals much about the belief structure of the services themselves. These beliefs speak to what staff assume about what children can do, the character of the children, and their potential.

Systems function independently (Hye-young et al., 2017). They support themselves. A system that is built on a structure focused on children's struggles – what is often called a deficit

DOI: 10.4324/9781003346012-7

model grounded in structural racism (Melvin et al., 2022) as discussed in Chapter 2 – will focus on weaknesses of children over and above their strengths. Such systemic beliefs seek to overlook the gifts and strengths of children often for similar racist reasons, when some educationists believe all children are gifted (Gardner, 2020). Any good educator will seek to simply identify and respect the gifts in each child (Perry, 2005).

ELNC has created a system of early childhood education (ECE), based on a clear, firm understanding of Ezeh and our community's beliefs about children. The ELNC system centers on the capacity of all children to learn and be successful in the future. This educational approach stems from the belief that poor Black and Brown children have power (Freire, 1970; Gutiérrez, 2006; Heath, 1983; hooks, 1994; Noguera, 2003). Chana Edmond-Verley calls this approach "scaffolding from strengths." "You don't have good footing if you are building upon a crumbling wall of deficits—if all you can see is deficits," she says.

> But if you can see the resilience and the agency and the propensity for a child to succeed, within the context of the environment and system they find themselves, that scaffolding creates a firm foundation for success for the child.

Edmond-Verley's comments reflect an educational view that children will rise to the expectations teachers set for children (Johnston et al., 2019). Whatever educators see in children is what children will show. What occurs in the learning space starts with the views teachers have about their learners (Ball, 2009). And ELNC, Edmond-Verley states, understands the context of learning shaped by educator beliefs so ELNC staff default to beliefs of the strengths in every child.

Melita Powell observes that the deficit approach has historically racist roots, as Chapter 2 lays out. Such an approach to education subscribes to the notion that children of color "lack," which unfortunately was part of the initial belief system that anchored the renowned early childhood federal Headstart program (Razfar & Gutiérrez, 2003) despite its anti-poverty goals. "When we're talking about children of color, it is a different battle altogether for them," she avers. Powell is aware of the importance of being honest about the challenges of marginalized children and the effects of racism. But she remarks that there are obligations of ELNC stakeholders to confess that "lack" or deficit is at the societal level and not at the level of the child (Iruka et al., 2022). Early childhood educators and society as a whole must be honest about vulnerabilities and disadvantages of large social structures and institutions that hamper advancement of certain segments of the United States population so as to design equitable learning solutions (Henward et al., 2021; Iruka, 2022). Part of the solution comes down to assuming that each child is an asset and not a liability. Each child has maximum potential. Anti-racist ECE assumes children of color possess at minimum all of the learning strengths of any child from any socio-economic background. Anti-racism drives ELNC teaching and learning.

To be clear, there are various theories of anti-racism, some of which have been popularized by the events of unarmed killing of Black people in the United States in the year 2020 that spurred worldwide Black Lives Matter protests (Henward et al., 2021). However, anti-racist scholarship has a long tradition whose deep vertical and horizontal conversation will not be fully captured in this book. Intellectual contributions from Sojourner Truth (Stanton et al., 1851), Ida B. Wells (1892), W. E. B. Du Bois (1903), Schomburg (1913), Marcus Garvey (1917), Carter G. Woodson (1933), C. R. L. James (1938), Franz Fanon (1952), John Oliver Killens (1954), James Baldwin (1963), Fannie Lou Hamer (1964), Alex La Guma (1968), Sonia Sanchez and D. Randall (1970), John Henry Clarke (1971), Evangeline Ward (1972), Walter Rodney (1972), Cheik Anta Diop (1974), Ama Ata Aidoo (1978), Angela Davis (1983), Ngugi wa Thiong'o (1986), Vivian Verdell Gordon (1987/1991), Patricia Hill Collins (1990), Charsee C. Lawrence-McIntyre (1993), Cornell West (1993), Claude Anderson (1994, 2001), Marimba Ani (1994), Edwidge Danticat (1994), June Jordan et al. (1995), Lisa Delpit (1995), to Jeanine Staples (2008), Keith Gilyard (2010), Vivian Yenika-Agbaw (2014), Umar Johnson

(2012), Gregg Carr (2017), Boyce Watkins (2016), Roland Martin, and L. Lakins (2022), Karen Hunter and N. H. Burroughs (2010) to newer voices such as Ibrahim Kendi (2019), Ijeoma Oluo (2019), Uju Anya (2017), Nkechi Taifa (2020), and Iheoma Iruka et al. (2022) from the fields of African, Africana, African-American, African Diaspora, Pan-African Studies, Black Studies, History, Literature, Journalism, Sociology, Finance, Law, and of course Education among others have marshaled in a host of ideas and frameworks on how to recognize racism and work against it.

Clearly, research on racism and how to undermine it is omnipresent. The question becomes what evidence exists that ELNC is in fact anti-racist? What in the organizational structure, early childhood programming, and pedagogy reveals that ELNC does in fact do anti-racist work? These questions have been answered in previous chapters with evidence such as the fact that majority of people of color hold leadership positions at ELNC, whereas some whites hold supportive roles, which is opposite of what one observes about most organizations. Or that ELNC operates in poor Black and Brown communities instead of busing Black and Brown children to white schools (Lenhoff et al., 2022). ELNC partners with Black and Latinx neighborhood community centers and churches. The parent teachers and family coaches serve as a form of racial/ethnic matching (Hanushek et al., 2005). These are all operational examples of how anti-racism is embedded into the organization.

These anti-racist beliefs, beliefs in strengths and capacity of poor Black and Brown children and their communities, are the starting point for all ELNC initiatives: every programming approach, every classroom design, every interaction with both children and parents extends anti-racist ECE. These beliefs guide the kinds of staff and teachers that ELNC brings into the organization to implement local neighborhood programming. These beliefs guide every step and decision.

Beyond her anti-racist beliefs, Dr. Nkechy Ekere Ezeh believes the following about children:

All children are born ready to learn

Each child is born with many strengths that grow as a child comes of age. It is an educator's responsibility to identify and use those strengths to help the child learn (NAEYC, 2020). Despite these strengths, adults developed structural barriers – ideally unintentionally and unknowingly – to the detriment of a child's learning capacity (Anning et al., 2008). Most children are not born with learning barriers, but many children encounter these barriers by the time they reach kindergarten (Bruckauf & Hayes, 2017). These barriers can be xenophobic, racist, and pro-poverty despite the natural learning power of each child (Oikonomidoy & Karam, 2022). These barriers are not natural. They are human made so they must be human undone. How does society un-do the educational damage society has inflicted on children? One response is to assume that poor children and Black and Brown children are ready to learn even before they enter classrooms. Assume poor children and Black and Brown children will be successful once they enter classrooms and after they exit them (Beteille et al., 2020). Children reflect the best of a society, but the structures adults have historically created for them may not be (Weyer, 2018).

Particularly from an education perspective, Ezeh's belief that all children are born ready to learn begs other questions: To what extent does the truism apply to children with developmental difficulties, particularly at the neuro-cognitive level? How do teachers educate learners with developmental challenges? Are such learners born ready to learn, even when they have severe cases of autism for example (Rozendal & Westbrook, 2018)? As mentioned above, Ezeh affirms the learning of all children, including those with developmental problems, as supported by research (Ching et al., 2020; Dhonsi, 2020; Ebrahim et al., 2013; Johnson, 2016; Leon, 2019). When Ezeh states that all children are born ready to learn, Ezeh means literally all children. Some will learn at their own pace, she explains, and perhaps very different than what are the expectations of the learning process for the general population (Beauchat et al., 2010). These children may have to learn in a different way, including with the help of an Individualized Education Plan (IEP) that may require any number of speech, behavioral, and other types of specialists but **all** children are born ready to, and will, learn.

Children are curious

Children are interested in the world around them and they want to make sense of it (Rothstein-Fisch, 2010). This curiosity is a particular strength of children, one that can be built upon to not only encourage learning and educational development but to encourage their *enjoyment* of learning. This affects, then, the approach to education for children, says Kathy Brower, former Executive Director for SECOM Ministries.

> "Everything we did was centered around self-sufficiency and empowerment of the child," says Brower. "Even when they would have lunch, they served out of common bowls and the children took care of it... they had to take responsibility for themselves. Everything had a place where it belonged, and children were an important part of keeping that environment in order and well taken care of. This worked to empower the children in creating that safe environment where they can explore and learn and be encouraged to do so."

Learning new things is *fun* for children, which is one of the reasons why "play" has become a staple in ECE pedagogy (Ferreira, 2021; Kishimoto, 2018). If we adults, too, approach learning as an enjoyable intellectual event of exploration of the world around us, such an attitude will be infectious – for adults as well as for children (Harris & Longobardi, 2020). Children are already inherently curious about, and interested in, making sense of the world. Adults should learn from children and vice versa (Kelly et al., 2021). Adults and children should explore.

Children have inherent capacity to solve their own problems

Children are *capable*. Early childhood educators such as Ezeh admit that play and other forms of pedagogy reveal just how capable children are at learning and problem-solving (Anderson-McNamee & Bailey, 2010; Jin & Moran, 2021; MacDonald et al., 2022). However, adult-imposed barriers, manifested in curricular and parental constraints, for example, may undercut the ability of children to problem solve (Ginsburg & Audley, 2020). Furthermore, a barrier-laden system works hard to convince society that children are barriers to their own learning when children are the solutions to societal problems. Societal systems protect themselves, often to the detriment of vulnerable children and their families (Pacchiano et al., 2018). But the truth is that every person, including every child, can solve their own problems at their level in their own way, particularly when quality education is accessible.

> "If you are able to survive in this crazy system in today's economics, and you still have a roof over your heads, and there is food on the table and your kids are dressed, you have got some serious skills," says Edmond-Verley. "So how do we create a support system for parents who are in survival mode, to give them a chance to dream about the possibilities for their child and their family?"

Clearly, Edmond-Verley is assigning blame where it belongs: with the social–economic system. The system that has put families into survival mode needs repair and not the families themselves (Essa & Burnham, 2019). Families may need resources, but they do not need repair, from the perspective of ELNC. Give families resources that they have historically been denied access to in a historically inequitable system. The state of ECE reveals that there is a learner access problem. But there is not a learner capacity problem (Weyer, 2018).

Children show us the future

What society provides for children is what society provides for its own future, according to Ezeh. The state of children is the state of the future (Karoly, 2016). If children are healthy, the future is healthy. If children are hungry, then the future is starving. If children lack resources to learn, then the future is under-resourced. If our children are not given opportunities to learn, then the future is not a learned one; the future will lack erudition. Children are indeed the future, as the popular maxim goes (Garcia et al., 2008). How society invests in future generations is how society invests in the future for everyone.

Accordingly, vigilance is key. Educators and other stakeholders must pay attention to the personalities, struggles, trials, and triumphs of children as evidence of investment in future progress or lack thereof. According to various multilateral agencies such as UNESCO (2021), OECD (2022), World Bank (Beteille et al., 2020), and World Health Organization (2018), the status of children is the best indicator of what adults are doing right and wrong. Children tell us what communities need to not just survive but to thrive. Quality ECE is just a basic right (Engdahl & Losso, 2019) to ensure that each community is of quality now and in the future as there is immediate and long-term return on investment (Save the Children, 2016).

Parents are the first teacher

Children are society's future, but parents are a child's first teacher (Barratt-Pugh et al., 2022). Parents are integral to children meeting learning expectations in the classroom (Varshney et al., 2020). Parents know their children better than any school teacher. Parents know how their child learns. Parents know their child's strengths. Parents are who the child looks to first to understand the world. School teachers are an important second teacher who must collaborate with parents if teachers aim to serve children in their classroom (Einarsdottir & Jónsdóttir, 2019).

The most powerful teacher is the parent. Only weak, unethical early child education programming will ignore the power of parents or will underuse them (Pacchiano et al., 2018). And quality early learning programming will center the child and his or her parents as much as they do the teacher (Gross et al., 2020). Parents will advocate for the best learning for their children and should be given plenty of opportunities to do so (Durand & Perez, 2013).

Deisy Madrigal says that this belief about parents affected decisions that were made long before ELNC opened classrooms. Parents were brought into conversations early, aware that their knowledge and insight would be needed to create success for children.

> You cannot have a successful program if you do it for yourself. The programming has to have the voice of the people that you are looking to help. So parents needed to be brought in so that we can learn what they know is important for their children, she declares.

Madrigal explains that this strategy requires setting aside cultural assumptions and learning from parents and communities themselves (Lee, 2013). The common misconception, for example, that Latino parents do not care about their children's education, notes Madrigal, comes not from the parents themselves but from an educational system that did not understand the culture of neighborhood learners (Crosnoe & Ansari, 2015; Schweitzer & Hughes, 2019). If schools fail to provide language services for parent–teacher conferences, for example, Madrigal points out that parents who are still learning English as their second (or third or fourth) language cannot understand what the teacher is saying. Historically, institutions blame families when families possess language skills that institutions don't (Souto-Manning et al., 2019). Why would parents attend and participate in educational programming for their own children when there are no viable means to participate? Language is communication and communication is participation, so one should not expect parental involvement at conferences, let alone willingness to select

ELNC or any preschool program, without the option of parents to use their own language (Ansari, 2017).

Children care. Parents care. Teachers care. Quality ECE programming will reflect this threefold system of care (Avornyo & Baker, 2021). Unfortunately, some early learning models may not be used to giving parents an equity stake in their own child's learning development. Models of early learning may not institute parents as an equity partner despite the overwhelming value of parents to teacher and learner success (Anthony & Ogg, 2019). Schools have to seek out the gifts in parents the way they do in children. If a school claims all children can learn, then they must hold the same view for parents. When a school values parents, the school's programming will speak to parental value. There will be systems put in place for parents to overcome barriers to language, transportation, and cultural differences.

Valuing parents also requires remembering *who* an educational program is created for in the first place. Programming should not be designed for ease for the educator but rather for the success of the student and his or her family. Such demands require a family-centric more than just a student-centric approach.

> "It wasn't a program for *us*," says Madrigal. "It was a program for them, for the families. So then we needed to listen to them; we needed to understand where they were coming from. Because that's the only way parents were going to trust us with their children. That's the most valuable thing that a parent can have—so we needed to make sure that they knew we were here for them."

The program was designed for families with children – for parents like "Brenda," a parent of an ELNC graduate. Brenda maintains that she feels more empowered after working with ELNC on her child's education. "Now I know how and **who to speak up to**," admits Brenda, getting to the heart of the resources needed for her advocacy. "You don't know what to say or who to even say it to, if you have any questions." ELNC, understanding the importance of empowerment of the parent, was able to offer resources and information that Brenda and all other parents should naturally get (NAEYC, 2020). This belief in the practice of parents as the first teacher also has long-term benefits for parents because their engagement in the learning of their child at ELNC sets them up for successful involvement in the primary education of their child as well (Kreider, 2002). In other words, parental involvement and engagement is an essential part of school readiness.

ELNC believes that the parent is the greatest resource for learning and ELNC's hyper-localized programming is evidence of such belief in parents. The family coaches, the parent teachers, the little schools or *La Escuelita*, and more are all examples of ELNC programming that foregrounds the power of parents for teacher and learner success (Raynal et al., 2021).

Children deserve the best

If the first teacher is the parent and the second teacher is the schoolteacher, then the third teacher is the environment (Guo, 2015; Jechura et al., 2016; Strong-Wilson & Ellis, 2007). Accordingly, one must not forget how setup of the learning environment impacts achievement (Callaghan, 2013; Curtis & Carter, 2014; Evans, 2006). Besides the physical learning space of an indoor classroom, environment includes structural phenomenon such as society, system, and community (Bronfenbrenner, 1979; Marchal-Gaillard et al., 2022). These all teach our children who they are, their value within larger sociological frameworks, and their unique place in the world.

The physical classroom itself is a powerful teacher for our children and reflects the level of pedagogical skill of an educator. The most vulnerable children deserve the best configuration of the classroom (Pacchiano et al., 2018), although research shows that "low instructional quality is disproportionally found in preschool classrooms serving low-income or otherwise at-risk children who stand to benefit the most from high-quality early learning programming and experience" (Pacchiano et al., 2018, p. 1). ELNC neighborhood children deserve to start at the same place as children in any other part of Grand Rapids, Michigan. ELNC learners deserve an environment where they can actually grow and learn. Kids deserve a learning space where they feel celebrated (Harley et al., 2007). As a result, ELNC classrooms are well preserved, newly furnished, kept clean, and decorated with everything needed to not just support learning but to explicitly communicate the idea that children are valuable, important, "worth it," as Ezeh's father would say (Ezeh, 2020).

References

Aidoo, A. A. (1978). *Our sister Killjoy or reflections from a back-eyed squint* (1st ed.). New York, London, Lagos: N. O. K. Publishers International.

Anderson, C. (1994). *Black labor, White wealth : The search for power and economic justice*. Gwinn, MI: Avery Color Studios.

Anderson, C. (2001). *Powernomics®: The national plan to empower Black America*. Gwinn, MI: Avery Color Studios.

Anderson-McNamee, J. K., & Bailey, S. J. (2010). The importance of play in early childhood development. *Montana State University Extention*, 4(10), 1–4.

Ani, M. (1994). *Yurugu: An African-centered critique of European cultural thought and behavior*. Africa World Press. Retrieved October 16, 2022 from http://books.google.com/books?id=IBxmAAAAMAAJ

Anning, A., Cullen, J., & Fleer, M. (2008). *Early childhood education: Society and culture*. Thousand Oaks, CA: Sage.

Ansari, A. (2017). The selection of preschool for immigrant and native-born Latino families in the United States. *Early Childhood Research Quarterly*, 41, 149–160.

Anthony, C. J., & Ogg, J. (2019). Parent involvement, approaches to learning, and student achievement: Examining longitudinal mediation. *Journal of School Psychology*, 34(4), 376–385.

Anya, U. (2017). *Racialized identities in second language learning: Speaking blackness in Brazil*. United Kingdom: Routledge.

Avornyo, E. A., & Baker, S. (2021). The role of play in children's learning: The perspective of Ghanaian early years stakeholders. *Early Years*, 41(2–3), 174–189.

Baldwin, J. (1963). *The fire next time*. New York, NY: Dial Press.

Ball, A. F. (2009, March). Toward a theory of generative change in culturally and linguistically complex classrooms. *American Educational Research Journal*, 46(1), 45–72.

Barratt-Pugh, C., Barblett, L., Knaus, M., Cahill, R., Hill, S., & Cooper, T. (2022). Supporting parents as their child's first teacher: Aboriginal parents' perceptions of kindilink. *Early Childhood Education Journal*, 50(6), 903–912.

Beauchat, K. A., Blamey, K. L., & Walpole, S. (2010). *The building blocks of preschool success*. Guilford, CT: Guilford Press.

Beteille, T., Tognatta, N., Riboud, M., & Nomura, S. (2020). *Ready to learn: Before school, in school, and beyond school in South Asia*. Washington, DC: Oxford University Press.

Bronfenbrenner, U. (1979). *The ecology of human development*. Cambridge, MA: Harvard University Press.

Bruckauf, Z., & Hayes, N. (2017). *Quality of childcare and pre-primary education: How do we measure it?* Innocenti Florence: UNICEF.

Callaghan, K. (2013). The environment is a teacher. In *Think, feel, act: Lessons from research about young children* (pp. 11–15). Ontario.

Ching, T., Harkus, S., Hou, S., Ward, M., Saetre-Turner, M., & Marnane, V. (2020). *PLUM and HATS: Helping to detect children with hearing loss from otitis media*. Sydney: Macquarie University.

Clarke, J. H., & Freedomways Associates. (1971). *Harlem : Voices from the soul of Black America* (Rev.). New York, NY: Collier Books.

Collins, P. H. (1990). *Black feminist thought: Knowledge consciousness and the politics of empowerment*. Crows Nest: Allen & Unwin.

Crosnoe, R., & Ansari, A. (2015). Latin American immigrant parents and their children's teachers in US early childhood education programmes. *International Journal of Psychology*, 50(6), 431–439.

Curtis, D., & Carter, M. (2014). *Designs for living and learning: Transforming early childhood environments*. Yorkton, CT, St Paul, MN: Redleaf Press.

Danticat, E. (1994). *Breath eyes memory*. New York, NY: Soho Press.

Davis, A. Y. (1983, February 12). *Women, race & class* (1st ed.). New York, NY: Knopf Doubleday Publishing Group.

Delpit, L. (1995). *Other people's children: Cultural conflict in the classroom*. New York, NY: New Press.

Dhonsi, T. K. (2020). *School readiness: Perspectives of early childhood educators* (Doctoral dissertation). East Lismore: Southern Cross University.

Diop, C. A. (1974). The *African origin of civilization: Myth or reality* (1st ed.). Brooklyn, NY: Lawrence Hill Books.

Du Bois, W. E. B. (1903). *The souls of black folk*. Chicago, IL: A. C. McClurg and Co.

Durand, T. M., & Perez, N. A. (2013). Continuity and variability in the parental involvement and advocacy beliefs of Latino families of young children: Finding the potential for a collective voice. *School Community Journal, 23*(1), 49–79.

Ebrahim, H., Seleti, J., & Dawes, A. (2013). Learning begins at birth: Improving access to early learning. *Early Childhood Research Quarterly, 21*, 153–157.

Einarsdottir, J., & Jónsdóttir, A. H. (2019). Parent-preschool partnership: Many levels of power. *Early Years, 39*(2), 175–189.

Engdahl, I., & Losso, M. (2019). The human rights of children and young people from the beginning: Early childhood care and education for all. In *Human rights for children and youth* (*Sociological Studies of Children and Youth*, Vol. 24, pp. 11–34). Emerald Publishing Limited, Bingley.

Essa, E. L., & Burnham, M. M. (2019). *Introduction to early childhood education*. Thousand Oaks, CA: Sage Publications.

Evans, G. W. (2006). Child development and the physical environment. *Annual Review of Psychology, 57*, 423–451.

Ezeh, N. (2020). *Nwaenyi: Child of an elephant: Lessons learned from my father, a Nigerian chief, about child development and affirmations*. Independently published.

Fanon, F. (1952). *Black skin, White masks*. France: Éditions du Seuil.

Ferreira, J. M. (2021). *Play-based and phenomenon-based approaches in the Finnish Early Childhood Education and Care*. Uberlândia: Olhares & Trilhas.

Freire, P. (1970). *Pedagogy of the oppressed*. New York, NY: Seabury Press.

Garcia, M. H., Pence, A., & Evans, J. (Eds.). (2008). *Africa's future, Africa's challenge: Early childhood care and development in Sub-Saharan Africa*. Washington, DC, Herndon, VA: Oxford University Press.

Gardner, D. (2020, February 7). All children are gifted—just in different ways. *The Seattle Times*. Retrieved October 4, 2022, from https://www.seattletimes.com/opinion/all-children-are-gifted-just-in-different-ways/

Garvey, M. (1917). *The Negro World. The Negro World Newspaper Collection, 1923–1925* [CEIML.NW.003]. Archives and Special Collections, Charles Evans Inniss Memorial Library, Medgar Evers College of the City University of New York, Brooklyn, NY.

Gilyard, K. (2010). *John Oliver Killens: A life of black literary activism*. Athens: University of Georgia Press.

Ginsburg, J. L., & Audley, S. (2020). "You don't Wanna teach little kids about climate change": Beliefs and barriers to sustainability education in early childhood. *International Journal of Early Childhood Environmental Education, 7*(3), 42–61.

Gordon, V. V. (1987/1991). *Black women feminism and black liberation: Which way?* Chicago, IL: Third World Press.

Gross, D., Bettencourt, A. F., Taylor, K., Francis, L., Bower, K., & Singleton, D. L. (2020). What is parent engagement in early learning? Depends who you ask. *Journal of Child and Family Studies, 29*(3), 747–760.

Guma, L. A. (1968, January 1). *A walk in the night and other stories* (1st ed.). Evanston, IL: Northwestern University Press.

Guo, K. (2015). Teacher knowledge, child interest and parent expectation: Factors influencing multicultural programs in an early childhood setting. *Australasian Journal of Early Childhood, 40*(1), 63–70.

Gutiérrez, K. D. (2006). White innocence: A framework and methodology for rethinking educational discourse and inquiry. *The International Journal of Learning: Annual Review, 12*(10), 223–230.

Hamer, F. L. (1964, August 22). *Fannie Lou Hamer's speech at the 1964 Democratic National Convention*. Fannie Lou Institute, COFO, Jackson, MS: Jackson State University.

Hanushek, E. A., Kain, J. F., O'Brien, D. M., & Rivkin, S. G. (2005). The market for teacher quality. Cambridge, MA: National Bureau of Economic Research. Retrieved from http://www.nber.org/papers/w11154.pdf

Harley, E., Perry, B., & Dockett, S. (2007). Early childhood educators celebrating and assessing young children's. *Journal of Australian Research in Early Childhood Education, 14*, 83–94.

Harris, Y. R., & Longobardi, C. (2020). How children learn from parents and parenting others in formal and informal settings: International and cultural perspectives. *Frontiers in Psychology, 11*, 1026.

Heath, S. B. (1983). *Ways with words: Language, life and work in communities and classrooms* (Cambridge Paperback Library, 1st ed.). Cambridge, MA: Cambridge University Press.

Henward, A. S., Lyu, S. R., & Jackson, Q. M. (2021, August). African American head start teachers' approaches to police play in the era of black lives matter. *Teachers College Record: The Voice of Scholarship in Education*, *123*(8), 86–113.

hooks, b. (1994). *Teaching to transgress*. New York, NY: Routledge.

Hunter, K., & Burroughs, N. H. (2010). *Stop being niggardly: And nine other things black people need to stop doing*. Gallery Books, South Orange, NJ: Karen Hunter Pub.

Hye-young, J., Byung-man, K., Mi-jin, K., Bo-soon, S., & You-jin, S. (2017). Complexity and early childhood education. 한국유아교육학회 정기학술발표논문집, *2017*(1), 174.

Iruka, I. U. (2022). Delivering on the promise of early childhood education for Black children: An equity strategy. *New Directions for Child and Adolescent Development*. https://doi.org/10.1002/cad.20483

Iruka, I. U., Gardner-Neblett, N., Telfer, N. A., Ibekwe-Okafor, N., Curenton, S. M., Sims, J., Sansbury, A. B., & Neblett, E. W. (2022). Effects of racism on child development: Advancing ant-racist developmental science. *Annual Review for Developmental Psychology*, *4*, 109–132.

James, C. L. R. (1938). *The Black Jacobins: Toussaint Louverture and the San Domingo Revolution*. London: Secker and Warburg.

Jechura, J., Wooldridge, D. G., Bertelsen, C., & Mayers, G. (2016). Exploration of early-childhood learning environments. *Delta Kappa Gamma Bulletin*, *82*(3), 9–16.

Jin, M., & Moran, M. J. (2021). Chinese and US preschool teachers' beliefs about children's cooperative problem-solving during play. *Early Childhood Education Journal*, *49*(3), 503–513.

Johnson, U. (2012). *Psycho-academic Holocaust: The Special Education and ADHD wars against black boys*. Philadelphia, PA: Prince of Pan-Africanism Publishing.

Johnson, L. B. (2016). *Assessing self-efficacy beliefs of students enrolled in early childhood education practicum movement courses*. Hampton, VA: Hampton University.

Johnston, O., Wildy, H., & Shand, J. (2019). A decade of teacher expectations research 2008–2018: Historical foundations, new developments, and future pathways. *Australian Journal of Education*, *63*(1), 44–73.

Jordan, J., Muller, L., Bright, S., & Poetry for the People (Organization). (1995). *June Jordan's poetry for the people: A revolutionary blueprint*. New York, NY: Routledge.

Karoly, L. A. (2016). The economic returns to early childhood education. *The Future of Children, 26*(2), 37–55.

Kelly, B., Devlin, M., Giffin, T., & Smith, J. (2021). Family learning online during lockdown in the UK. *Adults Learning Mathematics: An International Journal.* Newbury Park, CA: Sage Publishing.

Kendi, I. X. (2019). *Summary and discussions of how to be an antiracist by Ibram X. Kendi.* One World, UK: Growth Digest.

Killens, J. O. (1954). *Youngblood.* New York, NY: Dial Press.

Kishimoto, T. M. (2018). *Early childhood education schools in Brazil: Play and interculturality.* Sao Paulo: Tizuko Morchida Kishimoto, Sao Paulo University.

Kreider, H. (2002). *Getting parents "ready" for kindergarten: The role of early childhood education.* Cambridge, MA: Hardvard Family Research.

Lara-Cinisomo, S., Fuligni, A. S., Ritchie, S., Howes, C., & Karoly, L. (2007, October 25). Getting ready for school: An examination of early childhood educators' belief systems. *Early Childhood Education Journal, 35*(4), 343–349.

Lawrence-McIntyre, C. C. (1993). *Criminalizing a race: Free blacks during slavery.* Oyo: Kayode.

Lee, B. Y. (2013). Heritage language maintenance and cultural identity formation: The case of Korean immigrant parents and their children in the USA. *Early Child Development and Care, 183*(11), 1576–1588.

Lenhoff, S. W., Singer, J., Stokes, K., Mahowald, J. B., & Khawaja, S. (2022). Beyond the bus: Reconceptualizing school transportation for mobility justice. *Harvard Educational Review, 92*(3), 336–360.

Leon, K. (2019). *Joannie Busillo-Aguayo, Ed. D Date* (Doctoral dissertation), California State University, Northridge, CA.

Marchal-Gaillard, V., Marzin-Janvier, P., Boilevin, J. M., & Grimault-Leprince, A. (2022). Contribution of Early Childhood Education to a sustainable society: Influences from home in preschool children's understanding of composting in France. *Early Childhood Education Journal, 50*(7), 1247–1261.

Martin, R. S., & Lakins, L. (2022). *White fear: How the browning of America is making white folks lose their minds.* Dallas, TX: BenBella Books.

Melvin, S.A., Bromer, J., Iruka, I. U., Hallam, R., & Hustedt, J. (2022). *A transformative vision for the authentic inclusion of family child care in mixed-delivery PreK systems.* Chicago, IL: Erikson Institute.

National Association for the Education of Young Children. (2022). *Principles of child development and learning and implications that inform practice*. Retrieved October 15, 2022, from https://www.naeyc.org/resources/position-statements/dap/principles

Odom, S. L. (2016). The role of theory in early childhood special education and early intervention. In B. Reichow, B. Boyd, E. Barton, & S. Odom (Eds.), *Handbook of early childhood special education*. New York, NY: Springer, Cham.

OECD Education Policy Perspectives. (2022). *Quality assurance and improvement in the early education and care sector*, No. 55. Washington, DC: Directorate for Education and Skills.

Oikonomidoy, E., & Karam, F. (2022). Structural barriers and processes of defunding of funds of identity of refugee-background children. *Cambridge Journal of Education, 52*(5), 1–17.

Noguera, P. A. (2003). *City Schools and the American Dream: Reclaiming the promise of public education* (Multicultural Education Series, Reprint ed.). Dulles, VA: Teachers College Press.

Pacchiano, D. M., Wagner, M. R., Lewandowski, H., Ehrlich, S. B., & Stein, A. G. (2018). *Early education essentials: Illustrations of strong organizational practices in programs poised for improvement*. Chicago, IL: The Ounce of Prevention Fund and the University of Chicago Consortium on School Research.

Perry, B. D. (2005). Maltreatment and the developing child: How early childhood experience. *Centre for Children and Families in the Justice System*, 1–6.

Raynal, A., Lavigne, H., Goldstein, M., & Gutierrez, J. (2021, May 30). Starting with parents: Investigating a multi-generational, media-enhanced approach to support informal science learning for young children. *Early Childhood Education Journal, 50*(5), 879–889. https://doi.org/10.1007/s10643-021-01209-x

Razfar, A., & Gutiérrez, K. (2003). Reconceptualizing early childhood literacy: The sociocultural influence. In *Handbook of early childhood literacy* (pp. 34–47). Thousand Oaks, CA: SAGE.

Rodney, W. (1972). *How Europe underdeveloped Africa*. London: Bogle-L'Ouverture Publications.

Rozendal, M. S., & Westbrook, N. (2018). Understanding how the special education system works for students with autism spectrum disorder. In M. Wolff, B. Bridges, & T. Denczek (Eds.),

The complexity of autism spectrum disorders. NewYork, NY: Routledge.

Sanchez, S., & Randall, D. (1970, October 16). *We a BaddDDD People.* (1st ed.). Detroit, MI: Broadside Press.

Save the Children. (2016). *Power of philanthropy: Early childhood education.* Fairfield, CT: Save the Children.

Schomburg, A. A. (1913). *Racial integrity a plea for the establishment of a chair of Negro history in our schools and colleges, etc. [Leather Bound].* Indiana, USA: New South Wales: Generic.

Schweitzer, M., & Hughes, T. (2019). Does latent conflict resulting from deficit thinking among educators limit Latino success in early childhood programs? *eJEP: eJournal of Education Policy.*

Souto-Manning, M., Falk, B., López, D., Cruz, L. B., Bradt, N., Cardwell, N., McGowan, N., Perez, A., Rabadi-Raol, A., & Rollins, E. (2019). A transdisciplinary approach to equitable teaching in early childhood education. *Review of Research in Education, 43*(1), 249–276.

Stanton, E. C., Anthony, S. B., & Gage, M. J. (1851). *History of Woman Suffrage* (Vol. 1, (Rochester, NY: Charles Mann, 1887), p. 116; Salem, OH: Anti-Slavery Bugle.

Staples, J. M. (2008). "Hustle & Flow": A critical student and teacher-generated framework for re-authoring a representation of Black masculinity. *Educational Action Research, 16*(3), 377–390.

Strong-Wilson, T., & Ellis, J. (2007). Children and place: Reggio Emilia's environment as third teacher. *Theory into Practice, 46*(1), 40–47.

Taifa, N. (2020). Let's talk about reparations. *Columbia Journal of Race and Law, 10*(1). https://doi.org/10.7916/cjrl.v10i1.5182

Thiong'O, W. N. (1986, June 26). *Decolonising the mind: The politics of language in African literature.* Melton: James Currey Ltd/Heinemann.

Varshney, N., Lee, S., Temple, J. A., & Reynolds, A. J. (2020, October). Does early childhood education enhance parental school involvement in second grade? Evidence from Midwest Child-Parent Center Program. *Children and Youth Services Review, 117,* 105317.

Ward, E. H., & National Urban League. Educational Policy and Information Center. (1972). *The Young Black Child, His Early Education and Development: A Position Paper.* New York, NY: The League.

Watkins, B. D. (2016). *The new black power: A collection of essays by the people's scholar Dr. Boyce Watkins.* Your Black World Store California, CA: Createspace Interdependent Publishing Platform, Scott Valley.

Wells, I. B. (1892). *Southern Horrors: Lynch law in all its phases*. Memphis, TN: The New York Age Print.

Weyer, M. (2018, January). A fair start: Ensuring all students are ready to learn. In *National Conference of State Legislatures*. Retrieved from https://www.waterford.org/education/fair-start-ensuring-students-ready-learn/

Woodson, C. G. (1933, April 4). *The mis-education of the Negro*. New York, NY: Harper Collins.

World Health Organization. (2018). *Nurturing care for early childhood development: A framework for helping children survive and thrive to transform health and human potential*. Gener: World Health Organization.

Yenika-Agbaw, V. (2014). Black Cinderella: Multicultural literature and school curriculum. *Pedagogy, Culture and Society, 22*(2), 233–250.

7

Looking forward

Early Learning Neighborhood Collaborative (ELNC) had already increased the number of quality preschools manifold by 2016, just four years after implementation of programming in 2012. Results show ELNC added opportunity for 544 more children in 20 classrooms. Of these, 91% were labeled, based on assessments, as ready for kindergarten. Such figures reflect quite a reversal from the abysmal 2009 statistic mentioned in the introduction of this book revealing 83% were *not* kindergarten ready. In addition, ELNC met best practice standards for preschools set by National Association for the Education of Young Children (NAEYC, 2020) with a 100% success rate for all ELNC classrooms, in part by providing culturally appropriate environments that enabled kindergarten readiness (Souto-Manning et al., 2019). And ELNC plans to have additional evaluations as part of its internal on-going accountability structure.

All ELNC programs employ the Empowering Parents Impacting Children (EPIC) model, a dual generational approach based on the philosophy that the parents are the primary drivers of their child's education. The ELNC team has developed and executed a strategic advocacy plan at the state and local levels that includes parents as advocates (Harper, 2016; Rossetti et al., 2021; Royea & Appl, 2009). ELNC also developed and implemented an Infant and Toddler program (Essa & Burnham, 2019; Morrison et al., 2009) as an extension of the ELNC preschool program for 3- to 4-year-olds, which serves as opportunities for children to use to their full potential – from birth (World Health Organization, 2018).

The statistics noted above tell a story of the resilience of learners in the ELNC program. The statistics indicate that indeed removing structural barriers will lead to all children being ready to learn. The statistics convey that ELNC's structural form of anti-racism works. ELNC methodology overturns historical inequities. The numbers do not lie.

Consider the following excerpt of an executive summary written by Matthew Weyer (2018) for the National Conference of State Legislatures:

> Large gaps often exist in reading and math skills for low-income students or those of color when they enter kindergarten, and these gaps persist, if not widen, throughout the student's education...Research shows that high-quality early learning programs are significant in successfully preparing students for their education marathon. They often reduce retention rates and special education placements and improve graduation rates. The opposite is also true. When low-income students do not have access to high-quality early learning programs, they are more likely to drop out of school, never attend college, be arrested for a violent crime or become a teen parent.
>
> (p. 3)

The existence of ELNC and its success, based on the numbers, indicate that the organization is part of a societal solution that sends low-income students or those of color on a trajectory of academic and social success instead of social malaise.

ELNC has prevailed in the early learning space in part because of application of change theory or theories of change (Schindler et al., 2019). An important part of creating success or real change is ELNC's ability to take change theory and apply it to ELNC goals. Change theory is a planning, participation, and evaluation process designed to define goals and work backward to identify necessary preconditions for success. One must understand the root cause of the problem of inequities in access to

ECE and then proceed to change the systems producing the root problems. Change theory in this instance centers on changing systems and not children (Davis, 2012; Madondo, 2021). Many progressive educationists seek to fix schools because institutions, not children, are the problem.

ELNC's change theory is a "collaborative theory of change" (Vijayadevar et al., 2019). ELNC's framework offers developmentally and educationally sound steps that are non-whimsical, non-superficial because ELNC's framework stems from ECE theory and research, as well as from the professional and personal experiences of CEO, staff, parents, and children. ELNC remains open to and thrives on change insofar as change in programming is in the best interest of children and their families (Essa & Burnham, 2019). The goal of such change must be guided by helping children to grow up equipped to fully embrace their God-given potential as self-sufficient adults (Sosinsky, 2012). Preparation to be self-sufficient begins before school even starts to increase positive achievement results (Ritson, 2018).

As discussed in previous chapters, ELNC's collaborative theory of change starts with their two-generational approach and uses a shared service model of targeted outcomes. ELNC outcomes are threefold. The first two outcomes for the child and outcomes for the family go hand in hand with what the organization calls "shared service outcomes." All support services are child- and family-centered. This child and family-centeredness is also what drives data analysis and reporting, fund development, structures for food services and fiscal management. These aspects of the organizational operations also speak to nonprofit sector standards (López-Rodríguez, 2018). Child outcomes are more than test scores; they include coaching and mentoring and a creative curriculum approach (Horm et al., 2019).

But ELNC knew that these normative structures could not on their own create the change ELNC desired. Real change required integration of shared service outcomes such as indigenous leader development (Ezeh, 2022) and a teachers of color pipe-line. As such, in an effort to further buttress and expand, ELNC is undergoing a shift in leadership. Senior leadership is passing the torch to a new set of leaders in an effort to grow and develop indigenous leaders from within the community, further underscoring and living out the goals and mission of the collaborative. Those who take on the role of leaders within ELNC will grow as they learn, thus embodying the spirit of ELNC, which extends its ethos to include adults, as all adults have the capacity to learn. Furthermore, communities know how to solve their own problems, and by raising new leadership, ELNC will provide the resources and professional development to help adults reach their God-given potential to lead. Fortunately, how to lead and learn is the subject of a forthcoming project that will assist these new and talented individuals.**

Similarly, the family outcomes include progressive targets such as providing empowerment for parents to be change agents in their own communities.

**Here is where I was trying to find a clever way to plug your upcoming book, through Routledge lol. Might be a bit too ambitious. Please feel free to revise.

Because of threefold pedagogical leadership composed of parents, teachers, and environment, ELNC is able to increase neighborhood families' access to the high-quality early educational opportunities to address the needs of neighborhood children (Lara-Cinisomo et al., 2007; Figure 7.1).

Consider a report from a parent (who goes by the pseudonym of Francine) who gives a more complete picture of the true impact ELNC is making. "My son would insist on wearing his backpack even though there wasn't anything in it, and he would actually chant 'Pre-school! Pre-school!' as he entered the building," recalls Francine. "Over the weekend, he pretends to be his teacher and he teaches his stuffed animals what he's learned that week." Apparently, the educational experiences of Francine's son at ELNC are so impactful that he defaults to replicating these experiences at home. While some children may want to disengage from schooling activities once they are no longer at school (Farrugia & Busuttil, 2021), Francine's observation reveals the opposite here.

Francine claims the lessons in her son's ELNC-directed classrooms are reinforcing what she had been teaching him at home. "Hearing from someone else that we need to use our

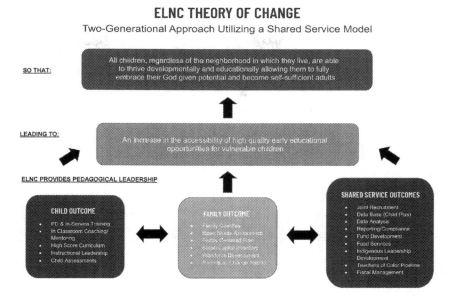

FIGURE 7.1 ELNC Collaborative Theory of Change: Two-Generational Approach.

words, that we need to be kind, that we need to be respectful," according to Francine, "was really helpful. I even saw development in his drawing skills…I was really impressed with how his fine motor skills developed, in ways that I don't think I could have done on my own." Francine's observations offer a case where the ELNC experience for a child is one where ELNC is an extension of the home environment and vice versa. In this case, ELNC reinforces the parental voice from home and the child brings the voice of the teacher back to the home because the parent and the teacher are on the same page, share the same values, have mutual cultural understanding, and more.

Because of the communal approach to education, Pastor Earle expresses he's become ELNC's biggest cheerleader.

> "The journey has just been remarkable, seeing it firsthand," the pastor conveys. "One of the biggest things is that we have been able to see a first generation graduation of any kind would be a preschool graduation. To see

those families celebrate their young children and that achievement, when they have parents who have never worn a cap and gown, is remarkable."

Pastor Earle marvels at how much ELNC has been able to do in a community that has been written off by society. Prior to ELNC, no other initiatives, programs, leaders, donors, and community figureheads had been able to bring about graduation to a neighborhood that does not experience ECE graduations in Grand Rapids. "We are a truly grassroots organization, built from the bottom up," he continues. "All of that speaks to the tenacity of Dr. Ezeh, to the collaborative spirit that we've cultivated, and to the commitment of the organizations to the people that we serve." Ezeh, according to Pastor Earle, is a big reason why so many in a community historically overlooked get to experience even a preschool graduation. From Ezeh's perspective, if children and families in the affluent, white parts of the city experience preschool graduations, children and families in poor, Black and Brown parts of the city should as well. The village is for all villagers – not just some.

ELNC plans to continue expanding and continually improving programming until every child in our impact communities has access to quality preschool education. School readiness, from an ELNC perspective, is for everyone. Every child must be given a firm foundation not just by parents but by community partners. This is why Ezeh's leadership has changed the narrative in the city, in part by being "hidden in plain view" (Diamond-Berry & Ezeh, 2020). She treats children of color as part of the Grand Rapids and West Michigan village. Ostensibly, such children will meet and exceed the expectations of their families and larger community when such children are acknowledged as actual members and treated accordingly.

Grand Rapids serves as the beginning of a long trajectory to provide hyper-localized early childhood programming in other city neighborhoods. ELNC has subsequently opened centers in Battle Creek and Kalamazoo because of the success of ELNC at the original Grand Rapids location (Miller, 2021). Racism and poverty are omnipresent, but they should not be. Looking forward, ELNC seeks to continue to attack racism and structural barriers that society imposes on children and families. Kathy Brower reminds us that the future of ELNCs in many other cities will become a reality. "We've always said children are our future. Well children are our NOW." Looking forward also means integrating new strategies to combat unforeseen events of recent past. The negative impacts of the COVID pandemic on children and families that were already struggling with embedded structural barriers that were in place pre-pandemic were multiplied. ELNC now must deal with a new current reality as we deal with the following threats:

1. An increase in the number of children coming into the classroom who are exhibiting social behaviors that require individualized attention.
2. A significant staff shortage in all areas but especially critical when classrooms can't open because there are no teachers.
3. Funding that has not kept pace with inflation and the current competitive wage market.

As we have in the past, we will deal with these threats through a collaborative problem-solving process that involves our parents, our staff, our partners, and key community leaders. We will need additional supports in classrooms so that teachers are not overwhelmed by the high needs of some children. We will need to increase our strategies around "Growing your own" so that a pipeline of ECE staff is constantly being developed. Finally, we will need to advocate to all funders, public and private, that the world we live in is different and therefore requires all of us to act differently so that in addition to the many deaths caused by COVID, the progress made in early childhood education is also not a casualty of the pandemic.

References

Davis, G. (2012). A documentary analysis of the use of leadership and change theory in changing practice in early years settings. *Early Years*, *32*(3), 266–276.

Diamond-Berry, K., & Ezeh, N. (2020). Early learning neighborhood collaborative: Hidden in plain view. *Zero to Three, 41*(1), 13–20.

Essa, E. L., & Burnham, M. M. (2019). *Introduction to early childhood education*. Los Angeles, CA: Sage Publications.

Ezeh, N. (2022). *Leading while learning* [Unpublished manuscript].

Farrugia, R. C., & Busuttil, L. (2021). Connections and disconnections between home and D we add kindergarten: A case study of a 4-year old child's digital practices and experiences in early childhood. *British Journal of Educational Technology, 52*(6), 2178–2191.

Harper, L. J. (2016). Supporting young children's transitions to school: Recommendations for families. *Early Childhood Education Journal, 44*(6), 653–659.

Horm, D. M., Kwon, K. A., & Laurin, D. E. (2019). Infant-toddler curriculum. In J. J. Mueller & N. File (Eds.), *Curriculum in Early Childhood Education: Re-examined, Reclaimed, Renewed* (p. 96). New York, NY: Routledge. https://doi.org/10.4324/9781315103310

Lara-Cinisomo, S., Fuligni, A. S., Ritchie, S., Howes, C., & Karoly, L. (2007). Getting ready for school: An examination of early childhood educators' belief systems. *Early Childhood Education Journal, 35*(4), 343–349. https://doi.org/10.1007/s10643-007-0215-2

López-Rodríguez, L. M. (2018). Nonprofit organization accountability: Compliance with governments, foundations, and corporate funder requirements. *Journal of the Grant Professionals Association, 16*(1), 44–58.

Madondo, F. (2021). Perceptions on curriculum implementation: A Case for rural Zimbabwean early childhood development teachers as agents of change. *Journal of Research in Childhood Education, 35*(3), 399–416.

Miller, K. (2021). *$12.4M grant aimed at expanding early education to Kalamazoo's underserved children*. Mlive. Retrieved September 27, 2022, from https://www.mlive.com/news/kalamazoo/2021/12/124m-grant-aimed-at-expanding-early-education-to-kalamazoos-underserved-children.html

Morrison, G., Woika, M. J., & Breffni, L. (2009). *Early childhood education*. Columbus, OH: Charles Merrill.

National Association for the Education of Young Children. (2020). *Principles of child development and learning and implications that inform practice*. Retrieved October 15, 2022, from https://www.naeyc.org/resources/position-statements/dap/principles

Ritson, L. (2018). Sustainability in early childhood development. *Educating Young Children: Learning and Teaching in the Early Childhood Years*, 24(3), 9–11.

Rossetti, Z., Burke, M. M., Rios, K., Tovar, J. A., Schraml-Block, K., Rivera, J. I., Cruz, J., & Lee, J. D. (2021). From individual to systemic advocacy: Parents as change agents. *Exceptionality*, 29(3), 232–247.

Royea, A. J., & Appl, D. J. (2009). Every voice matters: The importance of advocacy. *Early Childhood Education Journal*, 37(2), 89–91.

Schindler, H. S., McCoy, D. C., Fisher, P. A., & Shonkoff, J. P. (2019). A historical look at theories of change in early childhood education research. *Early Childhood Research Quarterly*, 48, 146–154.

Sosinsky, L. S. (2012). Childcare markets in the US: Supply and demand, quality and cost, and public policy. In *Childcare Markets* (pp. 131–152). Bristol: Policy Press.

Souto-Manning, M., Falk, B., López, D., Barros Cruz, L., Bradt, McGowan, N., Cardwell, N., Perez, A., Rabadi-Raol, A., & Rollins, E. (2019). A transdisciplinary approach to equitable teaching in early childhood education. *Review of Research in Education*, 43(1), 249–276.

Vijayadevar, S., Thornton, K., & Cherrington, S. (2019). Professional learning communities: Enhancing collaborative leadership in Singapore early childhood settings. *Contemporary Issues in Early Childhood*, 20(1), 79–92.

Weyer, M. (2018, January). A fair start: Ensuring all students are ready to learn. In *National Conference of State Legislatures*. Retrieved from https://www.waterford.org/education/fair-start-ensuring-students-ready-learn/

World Health Organization. (2018). *Nurturing care for early childhood development: A framework for helping children survive and thrive to transform health and human potential*. World Health Organization. https://nurturing-care.org/

Appendix A
About our founding collaborative partner organizations

Early Learning Neighborhood Collaborative leverages neighborhood based organizations to deliver services that support successful early education. Through the educational standards and technical support that ELNC provides, ELNC partners are empowered to deliver high - quality, impactful preschool and parent programs.

*Baxter Community Center, established in 1969, seeks to reveal God's love by responding to human needs in its community through effective programs and partnerships. Baxter's Child Development Center (CDC), is a dynamic place of growth and learning. The CDC cares for children from infancy to age twelve, including an ELNC Preschool program, allowing parents to work or attend school with the knowledge that their sons and daughters are safe. Dedicated to promoting the healthy development of children -- academically, socially, psychologically, and emotionally - the CDC helps to build foundations of learning that will equip children for future long - term success.

New Hope Baptist Church, established in 1934, defines itself by tireless and faithful service to the needs of humanity. Educating, Equipping, and Empowering are the three ministry imperatives that drive all of the organization's activity. New Hope has recently renovated space and is planning on housing two early childhood education classrooms in the future.

SECOM Resource Center (formerly South End Community Outreach Ministries), established in 1993, programs and services have evolved to address poverty in a holistic manner. SECOM's tagline "Helping today, building hope for tomorrow" describes their approach: helping today with basic, immediate needs, and building hope for tomorrow through focusing on health, education, and other root causes of poverty. ELNC Little Steps Preschool at SECOM, is a free, quality, and licensed preschool for vulnerable 3 and 4 year old children living in Grand Rapids.

Steepletown Neighborhood Services, established in 1993, mission is "to promote neighbor helping neighbor live with dignity and hope." Steepletown accomplishes this mission through creative programs and services, and by managing a neighborhood center that provides space to other agencies working on the West Side. ELNC Steepletown Preschool, is a free, quality, and licensed preschool for vulnerable 3 and 4 year old children living in Grand Rapids.

The Hispanic Center of Western Michigan, established in 1978, has offered the services that individuals and families in the community have needed to help them achieve self - sufficiency. At the basis of their success is a bilingual and bicultural staff that enables them to provide a culturally competent and responsive setting for Spanish - speaking clients. ELNC La Escuelita Preschool, managed by the Hispanic Center, is a free, bilingual, quality, and licensed preschool for vulnerable 3 and 4 year old children living in Grand Rapids.

***The Other Way Ministries,** established in 1967, is a Grand Rapids, Michigan, Westside urban outreach committed to Christian community development. Their strategic focus is Family Development: Walking alongside families as they set goals and seek growth through services, programs and leadership development centered around three pivotal areas: Spiritual, Relational and Economic.

***United Methodist Community House,** established in 1902, is a place where the community gravitates for its daily necessities. UMCH collaborates with area agencies to offer a range of family friendly programs, from childcare to family and senior. UMCH Child Development Center, employs a research - based curriculum utilizing best practices for early childhood development and includes an ELNC Preschool program. Children ages 0 - 5 can enroll at the CDC. The Center offers a qualified and caring staff, nutritious meals, and an enriching environment for children in this age group to grow and thrive.

PONA Consulting L3C

The sole purpose of PONA Consulting L.3.C. is to provide technical assistance to empower and support communities and organizations, who desire to create and implement inclusive strategies for the purpose of strengthening vulnerable and at risk children, families and neighborhoods living in poverty.

Early Learning Neighborhood Collaborative

Early Learning Neighborhood Collaborative (ELNC) is a trusted, place-based early learning collaborative that provides funding, innovative shared support services, and advocacy to partner organizations rooted in vulnerable communities. Through its successful dual-generation model, ELNC and its partners provide family support and high quality early childhood educational services to at-risk families through advocacy.

Note:

* Are no longer a part of the ELNC network. They still partner with ELNC to assure that children have access to quality early learning opportunity?

ELNC has added new partners: Refugee Education Center, YMCA of Grand Rapids, Grand Rapids Community College Phyllis Fratzke Early Childhood Learning Laboratory and Global Open Learning & Development Preschools.

About the community experts quoted in this book

Nadia Brigham

"Professionally and personally, children matter to me. I came from what would be considered a vulnerable environment and witnessed brilliance challenged and diminished daily. I have devoted my life to influencing the learning environments and structures surrounding children, particularly those made vulnerable by systems and structures that lead to racialized outcomes. I want children not only to learn to read and write, but to have access to their cultural assets that lead to wholeness and self-actualization. That is why ELNC is so impressive to me. It is not just about academic progress, which is certainly a powerful outcome of ELNC, but it is also about community determination over their children and leveraging the cultures of the children and families."

A former W.K. Kellogg Foundation Program Officer, Nadia Brigham is principal of Brigham Consulting, LLC with over 20 years of experience advancing racial equity, leadership and community engagement in philanthropy, youth-serving and grassroots organizations, particularly focused on racial equity, leadership development and community engagement for education justice, health equity, and family economic security. She's a strategist focused on moving leaders and organizations from awareness and knowledge acquisition to agency and action towards more equitable outcomes. Not secondarily, supporting leaders in examining and interrogating manifestations of internalized anti-Blackness and internalized superiority within themselves and creating pathways to healing is critical to her work.

Dr. Kimberly Diamond Berry

Dr. Kimberly Diamond-Berry joined the Michigan Association for Infant Mental Health (MI-AIMH) as Executive Director in

June of 2022. Diamond-Berry supports professional development, training, and attainment of the infant and early childhood mental health (IECMH) credential for IECMH professionals throughout the state of Michigan. Prior to joining MI-AIMH, Dr. Diamond-Berry led the research and practice arms at the HighScope Educational Research Foundation and was also Director of Policy, Grants, and the Demonstration Preschool. She co-teaches the Infant Mental Health Seminar in the Dual Title Program, Merrill Palmer Skillman Institute at Wayne State University. Dr. Diamond-Berry also worked at ZERO TO THREE as the Senior Technical Assistance Specialist with the Quality Improvement Center for Research-Based Infant-Toddler Court Teams (QIC-CT), and for the Early Head Start National Resource Center (EHS NRC). She has spent more than 30 years advocating, in various capacities, for the healthy development of children of all ages and their families through multicultural counseling, community psychology, private practice, and in early care and educational settings. She has lectured and been an adjunct professor of counseling and psychology at Loyola University Chicago, Northern Virginia Community College, and Bowie State University.

Dana Boals

Boals served as Vice President of Global Amway Brand/Corporate Citizenship and Vice President of International Finance where she gained invaluable expertise in leadership of global teams. Ms. Boals has also served as Director of Global Partnerships at Partners Worldwide, a global Christian network of business people faithfully pursuing a world without poverty. There she led a global team that built the capacity of Local Community Institutions to catalyze entrepreneurs and job creators in communities around the world. Ms. Boals' strengths in servant leadership, innovation, and strategic planning and execution, as well as tremendous compassion have significantly contributed to positive and lasting impact in companies and communities around the world.

Ms. Boals has transitioned from corporate leadership roles to that of entrepreneur and business owner in partnership with her husband. She remains active in a variety of community organizations serving on the Board for the Traverse City based Single MOMM organization, Grand Rapids based Early Learning Neighborhood Collaborative, and Chicago based Greenline Coffee and as Board Chairperson for Washington based Alliance for Children Everywhere.

Community parents

Quoted throughout the book are a variety of ELNC parents. Parents' voice is important to the ELNC work. Our parents are the first teachers for our community's children. ELNC parents are resilient, full of potential, and just need a little help to see their own potential. ELNC works to show them the potential they already have, empowering them and giving them the permission to make mistakes, grow, and learn as parents. But that potential is already there in our incredible ELNC parents.

Connecting parents to access to the tools they need is as important for their children's success as the child's access restoration. We've seen parents flourish as they navigate new skills and education. We've seen it best in them when we make our work with them a visual learning and growth experience, with explanations for why we are doing it and a chance to see what they may not have been given a chance to experience themselves as children.

Chana Edmond-Verley

Chana Edmond-Verley, Chief Executive Officer for Vibrant Futures believes in the power of agency, intelligence of systems, and wisdom of community. She brings to the forefront a focus on scalable solutions that leverage human potential, and create real opportunity for all. As a catalytic change-maker, systems-thinker, author and researcher, Chana has identified "institutions of trust" and "actionable information" as critical levers for achieving equitable results. A former foundation's senior program officer, her work and writings are featured in the Journal of the Economics of Education Review, National Public Radio (NPR), and Education Week to highlight a few. Chana holds degrees in Information Management (GVSU), and Economics (Spelman College). Chana is a proven leader with a passion for human potential, a great connectedness to the region, and a solid vision for expansion, and transformation.

Rev. Dr. Howard Earle Jr.

Rev. Howard C. Earle Jr. is the Senior Pastor of New Hope church. Since he has been serving in Grand Rapids, the ministry has flourished, a full time summer youth program was developed, partnerships with Grand Rapids Public Schools and the philanthropic community have been forged, and most importantly, souls have been added to the Kingdom.

Rev. Earle is actively involved in community affairs in Grand Rapids and Kent County. He currently is a board member of the Urban League of West Michigan and a commissioner for the Kent County First Steps initiative which oversees disbursement of funds levied from taxes for early childhood funding across the county. He also served on the partners' advisory council of the Early Learning Neighborhood Collaborative of Grand Rapids.

Prior to his current assignment at the New Hope church, he was a part of the pastoral staff of the New Faith Church in Houston, TX. During his tenure at New Faith, he served as Minister of High School Youth and Young Adults and Minister of Membership and Church Growth Initiatives.

K'Sandra Earle

K'Sandra Earle, M.Ed, currently serves as the Kentwood Public Schools Director of Early Childhood Education. Previously she served as the Associate Director of ELNC. While at ELNC, K'Sandra was instrumental in opening eighteen (18) preschool classrooms and ensuing that ELNC preschool sites maintain the highest quality. All of ELNC program sites have established and maintained at least a four (4) star rating from the State of Michigan Quality Tiered Rating System.

A self-described perfectionist, K'Sandra strived to ensure that each ELNC sites meet the quality standards that are held by the agency in terms of teacher qualifications and professional development with an emphasis on recruiting of teachers of color. She firmly believes that the staffing of an early childhood center should reflect the culture of the children attending the center. Early Education should be an enriching experience for the entire family.

Prior to her work with ELNC, K'Sandra was the center director at Baxter Child Development Center. During her tenure with Baxter she restructured the site's paradigm for early childhood programming.

Deisy Madrigal

Deisy Madrigal serves as the Program Development Manager at the Community Media Center where she uses her uses her extensive experience to develop ideas and grow culturally inclusive and sustainable programing. Deisy was previously the Director of Family Support Services at the Hispanic Center of Western Michigan providing overall direction and leadership for the Family Support Services Team. She was instrumental in the creation of the culturally specific and a culturally sensitive Domestic Violence program and Women's Program. She leads the Preschool, Adult Education, Basic Needs, Immigration, Domestic and Sexual Violence, and Mental Health programming teams and budget. Deisy has particular expertise and experience in the issues related to Cultural determinants in access to services for Latinos in West Michigan. She brings extensive knowledge and experience in infusing a holistic approach in developing programs for the Latino community. Deisy Madrigal is trilingual in English, Spanish, and French. She studied Criminal Justice and psychology and is a wife and a mother.

Melita Powell

Melita is the mother of 8 grown biracial children and that role created a continual learning experience as she discovered and lived with the realities of racial inequities. She is a passionate, culturally competent ally for communities of color, believing that the majority cultural must be willing to serve with and under leadership of color to change the realities of our society. She started serving with ELNC while she was the Director of Family Development at The Other Way Ministry. This role gave her a unique perspective as she sat at the table when the collaborative formulated its dreams and plans to engage in the work of providing early childhood educational opportunities to the communities most vulnerable children. Melita has served as co-chair of the ELNC Partner Advisory Board and when her work at the partner organization ended she did some contract work for ELNC facilitating and serving as site coordinator for a parent curriculum. She eventually joined the staff as the Program Assistant where she provided Administrative Support to the Associate Director and a wide variety of logistical and administrative support to the entire programming team.

Kurt Reppart

Kurt Reppart has lived, worked and worshipped in the 1st Ward for 18 years. The majority of his career has been spent in a variety of roles at The Other Way Ministries (TOWM), a neighborhood community development organization which has been seeking to empower families for over 50 years. He served as Executive Director of that organization for 5 years. He also spent 3 years working with a team in rural Honduras on a community-based healthcare initiatives.

Some of his current roles in the community are: West Fulton Business Association Board Member, GVSU Kirkoff College of Nursing Advisory Board, Neighborhood Match Fund Advisory Committee with the City of Grand Rapids, Friends of Grand

Rapids Parks Board of Directors, Energy Advisory Committee, City of Grand Rapids and Grand Rapids Public Schools Liaison Committee, South Division / Grandville Avenue Corridor Improvement Authority, Kent County Community Action Governing Board and West Michigan Works Governing Board.

A simple lunch with Dr. Nkechy Ekere Ezeh to discuss ELNC led to incredible growth for his organization- The Other Way Ministry who join ELNC as partner organization. Beginning with parent education The Other Way first ran the Proud Fathers program with connected with over 300 men. They then added the PREP program and over two years graduated 50 Latino parents from the program. Two years later TOWM partnered with ELNC to open an Infant & Toddler center called Little Lights providing slots for now 24 children. At each step ELNC helped The Other Way to build capacity and accommodate this incredible growth and has helped the organization make an even deeper impact on Grand Rapids Westside.

Rose Simmons, LMSW

Former Director of Senior Programs, United Michigan Community House, Rose Simmons, is a Solution-Focused Social Worker with over 15 years of experience, strong commitment to serving the needs of the disadvantaged who receive services in any given circumstance. She has a great sense of team leadership, program resource management, and the ability to demonstrate sensitivity to the population served. An adaptable and capable leader with strong work ethic, quality focus and passionate about serving.

Dr. Nkechy Ekere Ezeh

Dr. Nkechy Ekere Ezeh is an award-winning, international scholar, author, and educator. She is passionate about lifting up children and parents whom the educational system often fails. Dr. Ezeh's life centers on education, as she believes in using early childhood learning and authentic parent engagement to ensure that our community's most vulnerable children develop academically and otherwise.

Ezeh is a tenured professor at Aquinas College and the founder and pedagogical leader of the landmark Early Learning Neighborhood Collaborative (ELNC) – a trusted, place-based, early learning collaborative with affiliates in three Michigan cities – Grand Rapids, Battle Creek, and Kalamazoo. ELNC provides funding, innovative shared support services, and advocacy to partner organizations rooted in communities of poverty and racial strife. Through its successful two-generational model, ELNC and its partners provide family support and high-quality, culturally competent, early childhood educational services to at-risk families. Ezeh's life purpose is to ensure that teachers educate ALL children, which includes preparing Black and Brown learners for kindergarten achievement.

Dr. Ezeh's work has taken her across the globe to prepare teachers and caregivers, empower parents, and to testify before the state government as one of several advocacy strategies for poor children of color. Dr. Ezeh recently published her memoir – Nwaenyi: Child of an Elephant: Lessons Learned from My Father, a Nigerian Chief, about Child Development and Affirmations.

In addition to her myriad of professional accomplishments, Dr. Ezeh is enjoying a season of prolific academic writing, with two forthcoming books: *Providing Hyper-Localized Early Childhood Programming: A Framework from the Early Learning Neighborhood Collaborative (ELNC)* and *A Case for Developing Indigenous Leaders: Leading While Learning.*

BACK COVER:

Early Learning Neighborhood Collaborative (ELNC) is a trusted, place-based early learning collaborative that provides funding, innovative shared support services, and advocacy to partner organizations rooted in vulnerable communities. Through its successful dual-generation model, ELNC and its partners provide family support and high quality early childhood educational services to at-risk families through advocacy.

Appendix B
ELNC report card 2010–2015

2010-2015
REPORT CARD

Message from the CEO

Wow! Time flies when you are doing something that you are passionate about! I keep saying "pinch me"- is this all just a dream? Because that is just what it was five short years ago when the W.K. Kellogg Foundation approached me about facilitating a process to plan and design an intentional preschool system aimed at expanding the capacity of high quality early care and education programs in the vulnerable neighborhoods of Grand Rapids.

In simple words, Early Learning Neighborhood Collaborative (ELNC) was charged with the task of "getting neighborhood kids ready for kindergarten." When research showed that only two out of ten children entering kindergarten in the Grand Rapids Public School system were ready for kindergarten, we knew something needed to be done. At the same time, we also had to "get ELNC ready to get kids ready for kindergarten." So while we were planning preschools for our children, we were also establishing our organization and the ELNC preschool system.

How have we done? I will let you be the judge of that. Enjoy reading our very first Report Card and let us know your thoughts!

Thank you,
Dr. Nkechy Ekere Ezeh,
ELNC CEO

Dr. Nkechy Ekere Ezeh

Message from the Founding Board President

"You can do a lot by yourself but you can do the impossible with a great team."

Wise words that embody the spirit and impact of the Early Learning Neighborhood Collaborative, five years in. Confronted with the startling reality that fully 80% of children entering kindergarten from targeted neighborhoods in Grand Rapids were not equipped to be successful in kindergarten, ELNC was launched. As the founding Board President, I witnessed this collaborative of parents, families, institutions of trust, funders and early childhood experts set out to break through long-standing structural issues plaguing these neighborhoods that contributed to this dire statistic. The ELNC community was undeterred in their commitment to being the change agents needed to prepare these children for success in school.

We celebrate, on the five year anniversary of ELNC that over 1,000 children are ready to learn and excel as they enter kindergarten and we are equally energized with the prospect of continuing this work for our neighborhood's children and families well into the future!

Dana Boals

Thank you,
Dana Boals,
Founding Board President

OUR VISION

We envision a community where all children, regardless of the neighborhood in which they live, are able to thrive developmentally and educationally, allowing them to fully embrace their God-given potential and become self-sufficient adults.

OUR MISSION

The Early Learning Neighborhood Collaborative will create and provide targeted neighborhood collaborative partners with technical, developmental and educational support in order to increase the accessibility of early educational resources for vulnerable children.

OUR CORE VALUES

- Outcomes: Driven, results oriented - We must ensure our children develop and are educated, not by our good works, but by evidence of their increasing knowledge, skills and abilities.

- Cultural Competence: Children develop and grow best in ways that are consistent with the cultural rhythms and patterns of their families.

- Creativity and Innovation: Current efforts leave far too many children in under-resourced neighborhoods lagging behind in development and education. We must find and use new and different objectives, strategies, and activities to help our children thrive.

- Place-Based: We are committed to the belief that the best environment for the early education of children is rooted in what is local-the unique history, environment, culture, economy, literature, and art of a particular place-that is, in a child's own "place" or immediate schoolyard, neighborhood, town or community.

BOARD OF DIRECTORS

Leadership:
William Bennett - President
Otterbase, Inc. - CEO/Founder
Sandra Cole CPA - Treasurer
Edge Accounting - Accountant
Members:
Benjamin Amponsah - Member
Axios, Inc. - Human Resource Analyst
Liliana Garcia - Member
Chemical Bank - AVP/Branch Manager
Jordan Carson – Member
Wood TV 8/WOTV 4 Women - Co-Host
Andrew Vredenburg - Member
Foster Swift Collins & Smith - Attorney/Shareholder

Jackie Nickel - Vice-President
Amway - Chief Marketing Officer, Americas
Celeste Sanchez - Secretary
Spectrum Health - Community Health Educator

Dana Boals CPA - Member (Founding President)
Ferguson's Lawn Equipment, Fireplace and Stove Center - Owner
Misti Stanton - Member
Mercantile Bank - Diversity & Inclusion Officer
Preston Burrell - Member
Grand Rapids Drive - Account Executive, Business

Former Board Members:
Tatum Hawkins
Maribeth Wardrop

Nicole Notario-Risk

Eddie Rucker
Wendy Lewis-Jackson

Appendix B: ELNC report card 2010–2015 ◆ 163

ELNC PARTNER ORGANIZATIONS

Early Learning Neighborhood Collaborative leverages neighborhood based organizations to deliver services that support successful early education. Through the educational standards and technical support that ELNC provides, ELNC partners are empowered to deliver high-quality, impactful preschool and parent programs.

Baxter Community Center, established in 1969, seeks to reveal God's love by responding to human needs in its community through effective programs and partnerships. Baxter's Child Development Center (CDC), is a

dynamic place of growth and learning. The CDC cares for children from infancy to age twelve, including an ELNC Preschool program, allowing parents to work or attend school with the knowledge that their sons and daughters are safe. Dedicated to promoting the healthy development of children--academically, socially, psychologically, and emotionally-the CDC helps to build foundations of learning that will equip children for future long-term success.

New Hope Baptist Church, established in 1934, defines itself by tireless and faithful service to the needs of humanity. Educating, Equipping, and Empowering are the three ministry imperatives that drive all of the organization's activity. New Hope has recently renovated space and is planning on housing two early childhood education classrooms in the future.

SECOM Resource Center (formerly South End Community Outreach Ministries), established in 1993, programs and services have evolved to address poverty in a holistic manner. SECOM's tagline

"Helping today, building hope for tomorrow" describes their approach: helping today with basic, immediate needs, and building hope for tomorrow through focusing on health, education, and other root causes of poverty. ELNC Little Steps Preschool at SECOM, is a free, quality, and licensed preschool for vulnerable 3 and 4 year old children living in Grand Rapids.

Steepletown Neighborhood Services, established in 1993, mission is "to promote neighbor helping neighbor live with dignity and hope." Steepletown accomplishes this mission through creative programs and services, and by managing a neighborhood center that provides space to other agencies working on the West Side. ELNC Steepletown Preschool, is a free, quality, and licensed preschool for vulnerable 3 and 4 year old children living in Grand Rapids.

The Hispanic Center of Western Michigan, established in 1978, has offered the services that individuals and families in the community have needed to help them achieve self-sufficiency. At the basis of their success is a

bilingual and bicultural staff that enables them to provide a culturally competent and responsive setting for Spanish-speaking clients. ELNC La Escuelita Preschool, managed by the Hispanic Center, is a free, bilingual, quality, and licensed preschool for vulnerable 3 and 4 year old children living in Grand Rapids.

The Other Way Ministries, established in 1967, is a Grand Rapids, Michigan, Westside urban outreach committed to Christian community development. Their strategic focus is Family Development: Walking alongside families as they set goals and seek growth through services, programs and leadership development centered around three pivotal areas: Spiritual, Relational and Economic.

United Methodist Community House, established in 1902, is a place where the community gravitates for its

daily necessities. UMCH collaborates with area agencies to offer a range of family friendly programs, from childcare to family and senior. UMCH Child Development Center, employs a research-based curriculum utilizing best practices for early childhood development and includes an ELNC Preschool program. Children ages 0-5 can enroll at the CDC. The Center offers a qualified and caring staff, nutritious meals, and an enriching environment for children in this age group to grow and thrive.

PEOPLE WE SERVE

Neighborhoods

ELNC Zone Northwest (Westown Neighborhood)
Partners: Steepletown Neighborhood Services, The Other Way Ministries

ELNC Zone West (Roosevelt Park Neighborhood)
Partners: Early Learning Center, Hispanic Center of Western Michigan

ELNC Zone Central (Madison Area, South East Community)
Partners: United Methodist Community House, New Hope Baptist Church

ELNC Zone South (Garfield Park)
Partner: SECOM Resource Center

ELNC Zone East (South East End, Baxter, Eastown)
Partners: Baxter Community Center, Explore & Learn Academy (SEAC)

Ethnicity of Children

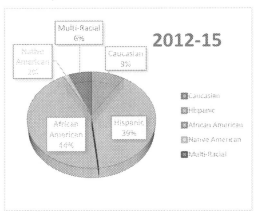

2012-15
- Caucasian 9%
- Hispanic 39%
- African American 44%
- Native American 2%
- Multi-Racial 6%

Grand Opening at SECOM

Parent Engagement activity – Learning about math while making gingerbread houses

Educational Achievement of Parents

On average, about two-thirds of our parents have not had educational opportunities past that of High School. ELNC makes every effort to reinforce with its parents the importance of education and provide them with the tools, support and encouragement they need to become the best they can be. This benefits not only the parents, but also their children, who are helped by a parent who better understands their role as their child's advocate.

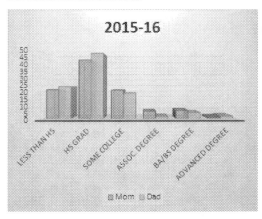
2015-16 (Mom, Dad) — Less than HS, HS Grad, Some College, Assoc Degree, BA/BS Degree, Advanced Degree

Appendix B: ELNC report card 2010–2015 ◆ 165

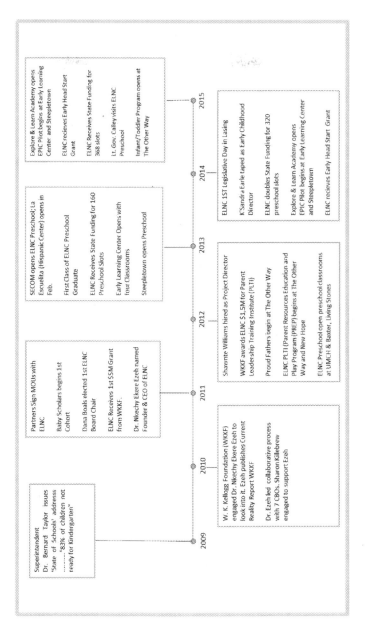

166 ◆ Appendix B: ELNC report card 2010–2015

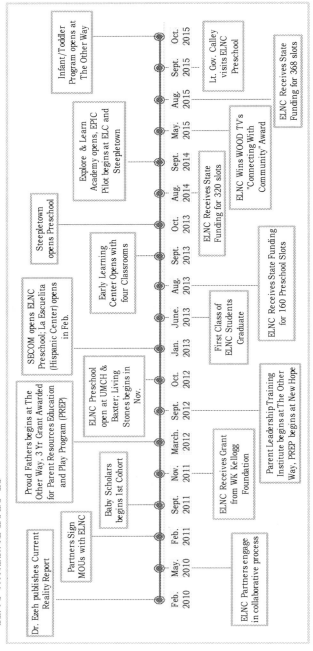

Appendix B: ELNC report card 2010–2015 ◆ 167

PROGRAMS – In Chronological Order

I Believe I Become - Baby Scholars

Through Believe 2 Become community meetings, local parents requested ways to help their children grow smarter. It was clear, parents were looking for real opportunities for students to become the people they aspire to be. To address this need, we partnered with two other local early childhood experts - Strong Beginnings and Arbor Circle - and Baby Scholars was born! Baby Scholars is an educational model designed to promote school readiness through preschool education and parent engagement. It includes: 10 weeks of preschool classes that meet twice a week for 2.5 hours, interactive workshops for children 5 months to 5 years, and home coaching for families with infants and toddlers. This proven model is based on the research of Dr. Susan Landry, a nationally recognized expert in parenting and early childhood. Dr. Landry is the founder and director of the Children's Learning Institute at University of Texas Health Science Center. Since the launch of the Baby Scholars program, 5,200 children have a stronger foundation for academic success.

▶ **352 Baby Scholar graduates enrolled in ELNC preschool programs from 2012 - 2015**

ELNC Preschools

In the fall of 2012, ELNC opened its first preschool classrooms. Every year since, additional classrooms have opened. Over the past four years, our growth has been phenomenal. In total, ELNC has 17 classrooms providing high-quality early education and care programs. All are intentionally located (in the neighborhoods where the children live) and culturally competent to best serve our target neighborhoods.

School Year	Total Children Served	Sites Added
2012/13	171	United Methodist Community House, Baxter Community Center & Living Stones Academy
2013/14	273	SECOM Resource Center, La Escuelita at San Juan Diego (Hispanic Center), Early Learning Center, Steepletown Neighborhood Services
2014/15	276	Explore & Learn Academy
2015/16	336	Little Lights at The Other Way Ministries

As a collaborative we set a goal that 75% of children who attend ELNC programs are assessed as ready for kindergarten upon completion of the program. According to the data, not only have our children met this goal collectively, but they have exceeded it in each area of development, including Social/Emotional, Gross and Fine Motor Skills, Cognitive, Literacy, Language and Mathematics. **91% of ELNC Preschool graduates last year had the foundation of learning necessary to enter Kindergarten!** This is a tremendous accomplishment considering that before ELNC was established, fewer than 20% of children entering Grand Rapids Public Schools were ready for kindergarten. **Our results are not surprising, given that all ELNC preschools have earned a 4 or 5 star rating from the State of Michigan Quality Preschool Rating Scale.**

Children served by ELNC preschools to date:

1,056!

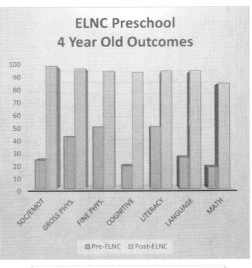

Appendix B: ELNC report card 2010–2015 ◆ 169

Parent Programs

ELNC considers parental involvement and support to be an essential element of a successful preschool experience. To better prepare parents for this role, parent engagement activities are offered at all preschool sites:
- Parent Engagement events
- Parent Conferences
- Curriculum Night
- Proud Fathers
- Parent Resources Education and Play Program
- Parent Leadership Training Institute
- Piloted Empowering Parents Impacting Children (EPIC) Model

Teacher Development

A focal area of ELNC is the development of Teachers of Color. ELNC Teachers are encouraged and supported to achieve their highest potential through various opportunities:
- Individual Professional Development Plans
- WOW! Fridays (monthly)
- Teacher Mentorship Program
- Leadership Series

Partner Capacity Building

ELNC has spent considerable time expanding Partner Agencies' capacity through technical assistance.
- Building ELNC Culture
- Working as a Collaborative
- Cultural Competency
- Grass Roots Advocacy Training

Community Awards

- Service to Children Award - Dr. Ezeh
- LINC Community Spirit Award
- Proud Father Facilitator Award from the State of Michigan
- Community Literacy Award for Inclusion
- WOOD TV 8 Connecting with Community Award
- Visionary Director of the Year award by the West Michigan Association for the Education of Young Children - K'Sandra Earle
- GIANT Award-Hattie Beverly Education Award - Dr. Ezeh
- Grand Valley State University Distinguished Alumni Award - Dr. Ezeh
- Hispanic Chamber of Commerce Non-profit Champion - Dr. Ezeh

The Esqueda Family's Story

Daniel Esqueda benefitted from two years of preschool at Early Learning Center (ELC), an Early Learning Neighborhood Collaborative preschool site. Before enrolling, "Danny didn't talk much and his doctor thought there were **speech concerns**," shared his mother, Maria Esqueda. Early Learning Center had just opened across the street, and Maria was hoping they could help.

When Daniel entered ELC, his assessment showed that he did not meet the widely held expectations for preschoolers in any area of development. He was not alone. **Before the fall of 2014, the number of children entering ELNC who did not meet preschool expectations was staggering:** 35% in Social-Emotional development, 76% in Physical development, 43% in Cognitive development, 38% in Literacy, 47% in Language development, and 35% in Mathematics.

Daniel's teachers, having participated in ELNC's professional development opportunities in math, literacy, observation and documentation, had a significant impact on Daniel's learning. He began talking more at home and at school. **His language skills increased and his doctor no longer had concerns regarding his speech and language development**. By the end of his second year, Daniel graduated prepared for kindergarten meeting all the widely held expectations. And he wasn't the only one. **Of children attending ELNC programs, almost all held the widely held expectations for development:** 96% for Social-Emotional development, 100% in Physical development, 93% in Cognitive development, 87% in Literacy, 85% in Language, and 85% in Mathematics.

Gains were not limited solely to Education. **The Esqueda family's social capital also increased because of ELNC.** "In my culture, the women did not go to school. I wanted to go to school but my father said, 'You're a girl. You will stay home with your mother.'" Maria wanted more.

Maria often offered to assist at Early Learning Center. Through her translating, anxious parents enrolling their children in preschool were put at ease. Her compassion and willingness to help, bridged the communication gap between staff and families at the center. The ELNC leadership team noticed this impact. This led to the creation of the Parent-Teacher position, and ELNC staff knew right away who the first Parent-Teacher should be.

Maria accepted and has been with ELC for over three years. "God put this opportunity in my way." Said Maria. "I told my mother and father that I'm working at a school." They asked, "Are you cleaning? " I answered, "No, I'm working with the children. I have demonstrated to my dad that I can! I'm strong. This job helped me to be strong!"

Maria continues to build her social capital. She is one of ten ELNC teachers completing 120 hours of professional development training in order to receive the Child Development Associate credential. **She also attends Grand Rapids Community College and is taking English classes.** "I love working with children. I want to be able to help other women and tell them, yes, you can. I did it and you can, too!"

All of this because Maria Esqueda walked across the street to enroll her son into preschool at ELC.

Appendix B: ELNC report card 2010–2015 ◆ 171

The Power of the Community! 2015 KEY HIGHLIGHTS
"Connecting with Community" Award
ELNC won the 2015 "Connecting with Community" Award from WOOD TV 8! Being acknowledged by the greater community for our achievements and involvement in our neighborhoods is an honor and something we are very proud of. For being chosen, ELNC received a yearlong 30 second public service announcement that will run on all of its stations including WOOD TV8, WOTV 4 and WXSP.

Graduation = Kindergarten Readiness
When the statistic came out in 2010 that 83% of children entering Grand Rapids Public Schools were not ready for kindergarten, it was clear that something needed to change. Dr. Ezeh and ELNC partners took on the challenge to prepare the children in their neighborhoods and put them on the right track to becoming successful adults. This past May, all seven ELNC partners took part in graduation ceremonies celebrating our students' achievements. Families came out in droves to watch their little ones walk across the stage in caps and gowns and receive their diplomas. For some families, this was the first graduation ceremony they'd ever attended. In total for 2014-15, 173 four year olds graduated from ELNC preschool programs. This is our biggest graduating class to date!

KaBOOM! Playground
KaBOOM!, a national non-profit, works with community-minded funders, like the Amway Corporation to bring balanced and active play into the daily lives of all children, particularly those growing up in poverty in America. On June 12, 2015, more than 300 volunteers from Amway, Chemical Bank, ELNC and the community volunteered to help build a state-of-the-art playground in six hours.

EPIC Roll Out

Parents who are struggling to meet their basic needs and have little social capital may have limited capacity and resources to act as a positive change agent for their children. Empowering Parents Impacting Children (EPIC) is a model developed to provide support, through the services of a Family Coach, to families as they identify and address barriers preventing them from meeting their basic

needs. The Family Coach also assists in the development of a Family Centered Social Capital building plan aimed at reducing barriers that impact a child's school attendance and threaten the family's ability to successfully complete their goals. ELNC has eight Family Coaches, with one located at each of our partner sites. The Family Coaches serve all of the parents of children currently enrolled in Early Childhood Education programs. Through the Basic Needs Assessment and Social Capital Inventory, the Family Coaches are able to determine where and how to meet parents in their situations as well as which resources to provide.

Lieutenant Governor of Michigan Visits ELNC

On September 14, Lieutenant Governor Brian Calley took time out of his busy schedule in Lansing to visit the Early Learning Center Preschool on Grand Rapids' southwest side. During his visit, Lt. Gov. Calley officially dedicated the new playground, talked to parents and, most importantly, spent time reading and playing with our preschoolers. As he left, he wished all of our preschoolers a Happy New School Year.

Infant / Toddler Program Grand Opening

"Little Lights" at The Other Way Ministries, ELNC's first Infant Toddler program, opened its doors to families in the Westown neighborhood of Grand Rapids on October 12, 2015. Little Lights opened their doors on the first day with a full roster and waiting list of interested families. The program operates year round, providing full day child care for infants, toddlers and two year olds in two classrooms, the caterpillar room and the butterfly room. The program has an overall maximum capacity of sixteen children, eight children in each room.

Participating families must meet eligibility requirements to enroll in the grant-funded Little Lights program. Eligibility is determined based on child and family need, as well as residential location. In addition to child care services, families also receive support from an EPIC (Empowering Parents Impacting Children) Family Coach.

FINANCIAL OVERVIEW
Summary of Income and Expenses

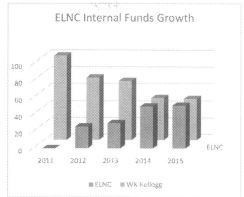

Over the past four years, ELNC has made great strides diversifying our funding base to include Public and Private Foundations, Businesses and Corporations, Family, Friends and Community as well as funds from the State and Federal government. In the beginning (2011), 100% of ELNC funding was provided by the W.K. Kellogg Foundation (WKKF). Since then, we have put much effort into our sustainability.

Budget	ELNC Internal	W.K. Kellogg
2012	26%	74%
2013	30%	70%
2014	50%	50%
2015	51%	49%

ELNC has reached out to many institutions and foundations to partner with us in our mission. Significant funders now include: Kent Intermediate School District, Kent County, Great Start Readiness Program, Doug and Maria DeVos Foundation, Steelcase Foundation, Frey Foundation, Keller Foundation, Sebastian Foundation, Tomberg Family Philanthropies, Cascade Engineering, Chemical Bank Foundation and Grand Rapids Community Foundation. We also appreciate the many individuals, small community businesses and churches who value what we do and have joined in our passion for helping vulnerable children and their families reach their full potential.

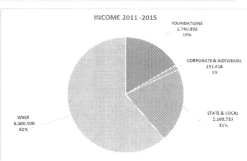

▶▶ ELNC Staff Members and the Board of Directors don't just talk the talk, they also walk the walk. Over the years, the board and staff have given very generously of their own time and money. Their contributions are reflected in the corporate and individuals total. This is a powerful statement of the level of dedication and commitment to ELNC's mission.

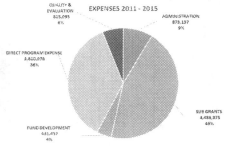

Message from the Current Board President

In 2010, when the W. K. Kellogg Foundation (WKKF) and Dr. Nkechy Ekere Ezeh crossed paths they discovered that they shared a common core belief - every child deserves a fair chance at success in school and life. Fortunately for the vulnerable children in Grand Rapids, WKKF recognized Dr. Ezeh as an emerging local leader who had a hard time accepting "No" as an answer and they made a strategic decision to invest in the fledgling, but innovative Early Learning Neighborhood Collaborative (ELNC).

William Bennett

In this Report Card you'll see just a snapshot of some of ELNC's exceptional achievements. We can't possibly capture them all, so we selected what we consider to be a showcase of accomplishments that are uniquely ELNC.

What lies ahead? Building on our momentum to reach even more children! ELNC has enjoyed incredible success since it began in 2010, but until all children in our neighborhoods enter kindergarten "ready to learn" there is still more to be done. As we enter our next phase, we will take what we do well and expand on it by making quality early learning opportunities accessible to vulnerable children at even younger ages. This will ensure our children are ready for kindergarten, and well-prepared for a lifetime of learning and future success!

All of our early childhood education programs will utilize our "Empowering Parents Impacting Children" (EPIC) Model, a duo generation approach focused on increasing capacity of parents to act as change agents for their children. This will help prepare parents for the important role they play in supporting their child's success.

Finally, ELNC understands that families have unique needs and for some center-based care does not fit well with their lifestyle. That is why we will invite home-based providers to join our ELNC Family, Friends & Neighbors (FFN) Provider Network. As members of FFN, they will have access to technical assistance, professional development and resources that will support them to take their early education services to the next level.

In closing, on behalf of the ELNC Board of Directors, I want to thank the ELNC Partners, Leadership Team, Staff and donors for their willingness to navigate uncharted waters so that vulnerable families can have access to high quality early learning. I can hardly wait for the sequel to this story to be told.

Thank you,
William Bennett, ELNC Board President

Appendix B: ELNC report card 2010–2015 ◆ 175

ELNC would like to officially thank

- W. K. Kellogg Foundation and the
- Doug & Maria DeVos Foundation

for providing the seed money that started this endeavor. Throughout this journey, other foundations have joined and supported our mission. We extend our thanks to them as well. They include:

- Amway ONE by ONE
- Cascade Engineering-Institute for Systemic Change
- Chemical Bank Foundation
- Frey Foundation
- Grand Rapids Community Foundation
- Keller Foundation
- Sebastian Foundation
- Steelcase Foundation
- Tomberg Family Philanthropies

Please consider joining ELNC and these foundation in preparing our children for a future of success! Frederick Douglas said it best,

"It is easier to build strong children than to repair broken men."

Date: _____

Gift Amount: $ _____

Yes! I would like to sponsor:

★ $150 (one child)

★ $300 (two children)

★ $450 (three children)

★ $600 (four children)

Any Amount is Appreciated

Early Learning Neighborhood Collaborative

Contact Information

Name: _____

Address: _____

City, State, Zip: _____

Phone: _____

Email: _____

Payment Method

☐ Please bill my: Visa / Master Card / Discover

CC Number: _____

Exp. Date: _____ Sec. Code: _____

☐ Check (payable to ELNC)

Online payment also available at www.elncgr.org

Signature: _____

LEARN. TEACH. GROW.

Baxter Community Center
935 Baxter St SE, Grand Rapids, MI 49506
Starr | starr@baxtercommunitycenter.org
616-456-8593

ELNC Early Learning Center
641 Vires St SW, Grand Rapids, MI 49503
Heidi | heidi@elncgr.org
616-323-3199

Explore & Learn Academy (SEAC)
1250 Sigsbee St SE, Grand Rapids, MI 49506
Cassandra | cassandra@elncgr.org
616-819-1406

La Escuelita
1650 Godfrey Ave SW, Wyoming, MI 49509
Deisy | dmadrigal@hispanic-center.org
616-742-0200

Little Steps (SECOM)
1545 Buchanan Ave SW, Grand Rapids, MI 49507
Amy | programs@secomministries.org
616-452-7684

Steepletown Preschool
671 Davis Ave NW, Grand Rapids, MI 49504
Kate | kate@steepletown.org
616-965-5825

United Methodist Community House
904 Sheldon Ave SE, Grand Rapids, MI 49507
Tamara | tamara@umchousegr.org
616-452-3226

Little Lights - The Other Way Ministries
839 Sibley St NW, Grand Rapids, MI 49504
Rachelle | rachelle.littlelights@theotherway.org
616-454-4011

Appendix B: ELNC report card 2010–2015 ◆ 177

Index

ability 16, 17
academic, expert 50, 53, 57, 60
academic performance 75
access 11, 14–18, 20, 23, 30, 34
achievement, cycles 11–13, 22
achievement gap 2, 5
advocacy 56, 59
Africana, African, African-American, African Diaspora Studies 112, 122
African-American kids 56
Aidoo, Ama Ata 121
All children are born ready to learn 123
All for Child Care 16
Anansi the Spider 94
Anderson, Claude 121
Ani, Marimba 121
anti-deficit 13
anti-poverty 121
anti-racist 92
anti-racist scholarship 121
Anya, Uju 122
autism 123

Baldwin, James 121
Bandura, Albert 108
barriers 19, 21, 35
barriers, xenophobic 123, 125, 128
Basic Needs Assessment (BNA) 86
basic right 126
Battle Creek 144
Baxter Community Center 12, 25, 27–28
Benson, Janice Hale 110
BF Skinner 107
Black families 17
Black immigrant 4
Black Lives Matter 121
Black Studies 122
Boals, Dana 2, 5

Bowlby, John 108
Boyer, E. L. 10
brain development 11
Brenda (parent) 128
Brigham, Nadia 18–19
Bronfenbrenner, Uri 108
Bronfenbrenner's ecological theory 113
Brower, Kathy 97
busing 5

Canada 16, 24
Carr, Gregg 122
Chall, J. S. 13
change theory or theories of change 140
chief 49, 55
child development 2
child development theory 15
childhood expert 68
child of an elephant 49
children deserve the best 129
Clarke, John Henry 121
classism 59
coalition 70
cognitive development 20, 22
cohort 85–86
collaborative 66, 69–72, 76–77
collaborative partners 57–58
collaborative theory of change 141, 143
Collins, Patricia Hill 121
community-based 20, 30, 34, 37
community-based organizations 67–69
community organizers 69
correlation 11
creativity and innovation 83, 86–87, 100
cross-sector 76
cultural assumptions 127

cultural competence 68
cultural context, assets 18, 20
culturalist 75
culturally competent 14, 20–21
culturally relevant environments 114
cultural norms, values 75, 83–86, 91, 93, 95–98, 100
culture 13, 23, 29
culture-centric 52

Danticat, Edwidge 121
Darwinian competition 70
data, collection, analysis 84–86
Davis, Angela 121
deficit, anti-, 13
deficit, theories 53
Delpit, Lisa 121
demography 51
developmental difficulties 123
developmentally appropriate practice (DAP) 106
diagnostic 85
DiAngelo, Robin 3
Diop, Cheik Anta 121
discrimination, anti- 19
disparity 4
diverse populations 76
donors 86

Earle Jr., Pastor Howard 3, 5
Ebony (parent) 97
economic security 114
Edmond-Verley, Chana 67, 74
83%, 9, 11, 14, 24
ELNC Partner Advisory Committee 56
Empowering Parents Impacting Children (EPIC) 139
English as their second (or third or fourth) language 127
enjoyment of learning 124
enrollment 85
entrepreneurship 57
Enugu 107
EPIC model 77–78
equitable, equity 16–18
equitable solution 95
equity-oriented 86

equity partner 128
equity stake 128
Erikson, Erik 108
erudition 126
evaluation 57
extended family members 92

family-centric 128
family coaches 23, 37, 88–90, 99
family studies 89
Fanon, Franz 121
federal government 12
financial partner 12
financial resources 75
financing 16
fine motor skills 143
folktales 94
Forbes 17
formative 85
foundation 11–13, 16, 18–19, 23–24, 26–27, 31–33, 36, 38
Francine (parent) 142–143
Freud, Sigmund 107
funders 4, 22, 34
funding, sources, strategy, needs 67–76, 78

Garvey, Marcus 121
genetics 13
Gesell, Arnold 107
Gilyard, Keith 121
graduation (rates) 5
graduation, rates, high school, four year 5, 9–10, 17, 20, 22, 29, 37
Grand Rapids 1–5
grassroots advocacy training 23
grassroots organizations 74, 76
GRPS 9, 24, 28
Gutierrez, Kris 53

Hamer, Fannie Lou 121
Head Start 53
high school 9, 20
Hispanic Center of West Michigan 12, 28
holistic 13, 15, 20
home language 94
human resources 58

Hunter, Karen 122
hyper-localized programming 129

immigrant 19
indigenous leader 4
Individualized Education
 Plan (IEP) 124
inequity 2
Infant and Toddler program 139
information processing theory 108
injustice 56
innovative 12, 51
institutions of trust 19, 22–23
Institutions of trust 67
integration(ist) 5
Iruka, Iheoma 122

Johnson, Umar 121
Jordan, June 121
justice-oriented 84

K-12, 11, 31
K-16, 52
Kalamazoo 144
Kendi, Ibrahim 122
Kent County, coordinating council 19
Kent Intermediate School District
 (KISD) 20–22
Killebrew, Sharon 2
Killens, John Oliver 121
kindergarten readiness 111
Kozol, Johnathan 1

Ladson-Billings, Gloria 53
La Escuelita 87, 90, 98
Lane-Zucker, Laurie 67
language 20–22
Latino neighborhood 92
Latino parents 127
Latinx cultural structures 92
leadership, dissent, executive,
 organizational 50–52, 55–57,
 58–61
leading while learning 56–57, 59
learning environment 129
learning theories 113
letter recognition 9
life-long learners 87

linguistic and racial minority
 students 53
literacy 2, 9–11, 20–22
longitudinal, foreword 9
long-term benefits 129
low-income 52
l'union fait la force 71, 73

Madrigal, Deisy 94, 97
Martina the Beautiful Cockroach 94
Martin, Roland 122
mathematics 20–22
maturationist approach 107
Michigan 50
multi-generational 20

NAEYC 13
National Association for the
 Education of Young Children
 112, 119, 139
National Conference of State
 Legislatures 140
natural selection 70
New Hope Baptist Church 12, 25, 27,
 29, 96
Nigeria 4
nonprofit 58, 141

OECD 16
Oluo, Ijeoma 3, 122
Onyinyé MK 109, 110
organizational operations 141
organizational roadmap 59
The Other Way Ministries 10, 12, 15,
 25, 27, 29, 33
outcomes 11, 19

paradigms 5
parental confidence 67
parental engagement, involvement
 12–13, 22
parental involvement 74–76
parental involvement, engagement
 12–13, 18, 22, 33
parent programs 22
parents are the first teacher 126
parent teachers 88, 90, 92, 99
partner capacity building 23

Pavlov, Ivan 107
people of color 60
philanthropists 77
philanthropy 70
phonological 9
physical classroom 129
physical development 20, 22
Piaget, Jean 107
place-based 20, 34, 66–67, 72
post-assessments 85
potential, foreword 3, 10, 12–13, 17, 23
poverty 1–3, 11, 17, 24
poverty, foreword 1–3
Powell, Melita 57, 59
power 12, 17, 20–21, 23, 29
power players 69
pre-assessment 85
predictors of educational achievement 89
pre-K 22
pre-kindergarten 22
prenatal experience 76, 106–108, 110–114
preparation gap 2
preschool 10–13, 15–16, 20, 25–31, 33, 38–40
primary, preface 9, 12, 20–21, 22
principle 13
proficient 9
profit and loss statements 69
Program Manager at The Other Way Ministries 57
programming, hyper-localized 1, 4
project manager 99
public good 16, 22

quality preschools 139

race 11, 17, 20
race, racial equity 11, 17–18, 20
racial and ethnic matching 92
racialized 60
racialized landscape 17
racism 1–4, 59
racist 13
relationship-building 68, 77
remediation 10

Reppart, Kurt 15, 25
representation 19
resources 5
return on investment 126
Rodney, Walter 121

Sanchez, Sonia 121
scarcity mentality 70, 72
Schomburg, A. A. 121
school readiness 22, 111
SECOM Ministries 97
SECOM Resource Center 27
secondary 10
segregation 1–4
self-sufficiency 124
self-sufficient 10, 12
Shirley Brice Heath 53
Simmons, Rose 55, 71
social capital 78, 89
social-emotional development 22
social justice 11, 18, 22
social work 89
societal hierarchy 60
socio-economic 12, 17
Sojourner Truth 121
staffing, decision 57–60
stakeholders 11–12, 17–19, 34, 66, 69, 76–77
Staples, Jeanine 121
startup, company 57, 60
State of Michigan 12, 21, 86, 91
State of Michigan Quality Preschool Rating Scale 21
Steepletown Neighborhood Services 12, 25, 34
strengths-modeled 20
structural barriers, inequalities, inequities 2–4
structural racism 120
struggles for existence 70
struggling learners 1
student-centric 128
summative 85
systemic 13, 16–17
systems 50

Taifa, Nkechi 122
targeted assistance 89

Taylor, Bernard 9, 24
teacher development 23
teachers of color 92
tenacity 12
territorial 70, 72
testimony 52
Thiong'o, Ngugi wa 121
threefold system of care 128
transportation 74
transportation, barrier 74, 78, 87, 95, 97
two-generation 77
two-generational 12–13

unconscious urges 107
UNESCO 126
United Methodist Community House 12, 25, 27–28

values 49–50, 54–56, 61
Verdell, Vivian 121
village 49, 52, 54, 61
vision 12, 13, 14, 26
Visions for Children 110
visual meaning 9
visual world 1

vulnerable, communities, children 11–12, 14–15, 17–19, 24–25, 31, 34–35, 37, 39
vulnerable, neighborhood 11–12, 14–18, 20, 24–25, 30–31, 34–35, 37
Vygotsky, Lev 107

Ward, Evangeline 121
War on Poverty 53
Watkins, Boyce 122
Watson, John 107
West, Cornell 121
West Michigan Nice 19
White children 92–93
whiteness 3
white skin 17
W.K. Kellogg Foundation 24, 26, 31, 33
Woodson, Carter G. 121
World Bank 126
World Health Organization 111–112

Yenika-Agbaw, Vivian 121

zip code 5

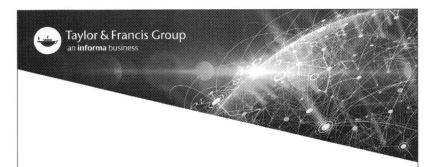

Printed in the United States
by Baker & Taylor Publisher Services